T0358341

Cambridge Elements

Elements in Language Teaching
edited by
Heath Rose
University of Oxford
Jim McKinley
University College London

WILLINGNESS TO COMMUNICATE IN A SECOND LANGUAGE

Jian-E Peng
Shantou University

CAMBRIDGE
UNIVERSITY PRESS

Shaftesbury Road, Cambridge CB2 8EA, United Kingdom

One Liberty Plaza, 20th Floor, New York, NY 10006, USA

477 Williamstown Road, Port Melbourne, VIC 3207, Australia

314–321, 3rd Floor, Plot 3, Splendor Forum, Jasola District Centre, New Delhi – 110025, India

103 Penang Road, #05–06/07, Visioncrest Commercial, Singapore 238467

Cambridge University Press is part of Cambridge University Press & Assessment, a department of the University of Cambridge.

We share the University's mission to contribute to society through the pursuit of education, learning and research at the highest international levels of excellence.

www.cambridge.org
Information on this title: www.cambridge.org/9781009539432

DOI: 10.1017/9781009417884

First published 2025

A catalogue record for this publication is available from the British Library

ISBN 978-1-009-53943-2 Hardback
ISBN 978-1-009-41786-0 Paperback
ISSN 2632-4415 (online)
ISSN 2632-4407 (print)

Willingness to Communicate in a Second Language

Elements in Language Teaching

DOI: 10.1017/9781009417884
First published online: January 2025

Jian-E Peng
Shantou University
Author for correspondence: Jian-E Peng, pengjiane@stu.edu.cn

Abstract: This Element offers a review of research advancements in willingness to communicate (WTC) in a second language (L2) over the past twenty-five years. It begins with the origin of the concept of WTC in first language (L1) communication research and the seminal and novel conceptualizations of WTC in the L2 context. This Element then categorizes six key perspectives that have informed WTC research: social psychological, cultural, dynamic, ecological, multimodal, and digital. By analyzing representative studies, it elucidates insights gained from these perspectives. The Element then discusses key factors associated with WTC, including individual attributes, situational factors, and outcome factors. This is followed by an overview of and critical commentary on methodological approaches in WTC research. Implications for enhancing L2 learners' WTC in in-class, out-of-class, and digital contexts are discussed. The Element concludes by proposing important venues for future WTC research. This title is also available as Open Access on Cambridge Core.

This Element also has a video abstract: www.cambridge.org/ELAT_Peng

Keywords: willingness to communicate (WTC), second language (L2), dynamic perspective, digital perspective, ecological perspective

ISBNs: 9781009539432 (HB), 9781009417860 (PB), 9781009417884 (OC)
ISSNs: 2632-4415 (online), 2632-4407 (print)

Contents

1 Introduction

Second language (L2) learning generally entails frequent and sufficient communication for learners to savor authentic use of the target language in various situations. However, L2 learners, including those having high L2 proficiency, are often observed to be removed from L2 communication in formal educational contexts (Cao, 2014) or naturalistic settings (Denies et al., 2015). This phenomenon suggests that L2 learners' language proficiency does not necessarily translate into actual communicative action, and for this to happen, learners' willingness to do so should be an essential prerequisite (Dörnyei, 2005). Hence, L2 learners' willingness to communicate (WTC) has been a focus of scholarly interest for more than two decades. WTC in an L2 is viewed as learners' readiness to communicate using the L2 in particular settings, which is an antecedent of L2 use (MacIntyre et al., 1998). Therefore, creating L2 WTC among learners is argued to be of paramount importance in L2 education.

Individuals' WTC is an intriguing construct that is not readily deciphered. For example, one's WTC in the first language (L1) is considered personality-based, meaning that an individual tends to demonstrate relative stability in their inclination to talk (McCroskey & Baer, 1985). However, L2 WTC (henceforth WTC, in contrast to L1 WTC) is conceptualized as a situated construct that encompasses both trait and state characteristics (Dörnyei, 2005). MacIntyre et al.'s (1998) seminal work marks the milestone of WTC research. They advanced a pyramid-shaped model that integrates a range of linguistic, communicative, and social psychological factors that influence WTC. This model has laid the groundwork for numerous subsequent studies.

A growing body of research has demonstrated the situated nature of WTC. Second language learners' WTC has been revealed to be subject to the influences of factors both internal to learners, such as their L2 learning motivation and attitudes (Yashima, 2002), emotions (Khajavy et al., 2018), and beliefs (Fushino, 2010), and external factors such as classroom environment (Peng & Woodrow, 2010), interactional context (Cao & Philp, 2006), and metacognitive instruction (Sato & Dussuel Lam, 2021). The WTC research has gained further momentum with the incorporation of broader theoretical perspectives, such as the complex dynamic systems theory (CDST; MacIntyre & Legatto, 2011) and ecological perspectives (Peng, 2012), as well as the inclusion of digital contexts (Lee & Drajati, 2020). The growing research interest in WTC is most evidently reflected in two recent book chapters that review the body of WTC research (Peng, 2022; Yashima, 2022). In brief, from its inception, WTC research has been continually thriving and new studies with various foci have emerged. Given this expansion, a thorough and state-of-the-art review of the depth and breadth of WTC research conducted over the past two-plus decades is timely, which will not only provide a comprehensive understanding of the field but also shed light on potential future research.

This Element is structured into six sections. In Section 1, the origin of the concept of WTC and its conceptualizations are introduced. Section 2 introduces the diverse perspectives adopted for approaching WTC, beginning with a social psychological perspective in its early stages and evolving to include the most recent digital perspective. Section 3 presents an extensive review of the factors associated with WTC, encompassing individual attributes, situational factors, and outcome factors. Section 4 details methodological approaches used to elicit data and analyze data in this area. Subsequently, Sections 5 and 6 discuss practical implications for enhancing L2 learners' WTC and propose directions for future research.

2 WTC in an L2: Seminal and Novel Conceptualizations

It seems intuitive that L2 learners' willingness to talk is a prerequisite for actual talking. Therefore, since its introduction, WTC has been recognized as a construct beneficial to L2 learners' language development. This concept aligns inherently with the principles behind communicative language teaching, which emphasizes the importance of engaging learners in meaningful communication practice (Littlewood, 1981). In this section, the concept of WTC is first introduced, and its conceptualizations and operationalizations in the L2 field are then expounded.

2.1 The Origin of the Concept of WTC

The concept of WTC has its roots in L1 communication research. It was developed from earlier three related notions: *unwillingness to communicate* (Burgoon, 1976), *predisposition toward verbal behavior* (Mortensen et al., 1977), and *shyness* (McCroskey & Richmond, 1982). Unwillingness to communicate is taken as a global communication construct that reflects "a chronic tendency to avoid and/or devalue oral communication" (Burgoon, 1976, p. 60). Predisposition toward verbal behavior is described as a person's characteristic disposition to speak that shows cross-situational consistency. Shyness is defined as "the tendency to be timid, reserved, and most specifically, talk less" (McCroskey & Richmond, 1982, p. 460). Based on these predecessors, the construct of WTC in L1 communication research was proposed by McCroskey and Baer (1985) to denote an individual's inclination to talk with others when given free choice. First language WTC is argued to be a "personality-based, traitlike predisposition" (McCroskey & Richmond, 1987, p. 134), meaning that an individual's levels of

L1 WTC in various situations and with various interlocutors tend to be correlated. Notably, L1 WTC is believed to be primarily linked to personality traits, as speaking proficiency is not a concern in the L1 setting. This contrasts fundamentally with the case of WTC in L2, where learners' proficiency can range from extremely low to substantially high.

Besides its trait-like nature, the cognitive nature of L1 WTC, being a volitional act, is also recognized (McCroskey & Richmond, 1991). This means that individuals have the ability to choose whether to talk. Such volitional choice is often influenced by the individual's personality. First language communication research has shown that factors such as introversion, anomie and alienation, self-esteem, communication competence, and communication apprehension are antecedents of L1 WTC (McCroskey & Richmond, 1991).

In addition, cultural divergence can influence individuals' L1 WTC (McCroskey & Richmond, 1991). For instance, as noted by McCroskey and Richmond (1991), interpersonal communication is highly valued in the North American culture to the extent that how much one communicates is related to how positively one is evaluated. This is different from some cultures where silence sometimes is valued as a ritual and respect for others (Liu, 2002). Hence, McCroskey and Richmond (1991) pointed out that an individual's willingness to communicate is highly related to the culture where they reside.

In the educational context, L1 WTC inside the classroom has been found to be associated with classroom factors (McCroskey & McCroskey, 2002). With a specific focus on the classroom, McCroskey and McCroskey (2002) discussed situational constraints on L1 WTC. For instance, students' L1 WTC may be reduced if the teacher is not supportive or is judgmental of students' talk. Disinterest in the subject matter or a negative disposition towards the instructor can also hinder students' L1 WTC. These propositions are resonant in numerous findings in WTC research in the L2 field, which are detailed in Section 4.

2.2 Conceptualizations of L2 WTC

The notion of WTC in L1 communication research was soon introduced to the L2 field, given the importance of talking in order to learn (Skehan, 1989) shared by the L2 research community. The WTC research was initiated by MacIntyre and Charos (1996) who studied the relationships between WTC, personality traits, perceived competence, L2 anxiety, motivation, and L2 communication frequency. Their study validated the integration of factors from SLA with those from the communication domain. It empirically established WTC as a significant variable in L2 learning, setting the paradigm for WTC research that frequently incorporates multiple factors and quantitatively assesses their interrelationships.

In contrast to L1 WTC which was treated as a personality trait, WTC was conceptualized to comprise both trait and state characteristics, emphasizing both constancy and situational variations in learners' inclination to engage in L2 communication. This is particularly because learners' L2 proficiency can vary hugely, leading to different WTC levels across situations. Willingness to communicate was defined as "a readiness to enter into discourse at a particular time with a specific person or persons, using a L2" (MacIntyre et al., 1998, p. 547). MacIntyre et al.'s (1998) model of variables influencing WTC (Figure 1) is the seminal work that has laid the theoretical foundations for WTC research in the subsequent decades.

This model illustrates the variables purported to exert enduring influences (variables in Layers IV to VI) and transient influences (variables in Layer III) on WTC. Moving from the bottom to the top, variables in each layer serve as the foundation for the variables in the layer above. The social and individual context (Level VI) contains intergroup climate (Box 11, the intergroup climate of a community and attitudes toward the L2 community) and personality (Box 12). The influences of these elements are most long-term and stable. The affective-cognitive context (Layer V) concerns intergroup attitudes (Box 8, e.g., integrativeness), social situation (Box 9, e.g., interlocutors), and communicative competence (Box 10). Layer IV involves motivational propensities including interpersonal motivation (Box 5), intergroup motivation (Box 6), and L2 self-confidence (Box 7), the former two are related to learners' intentions to assert control or establish connections at personal and group levels,

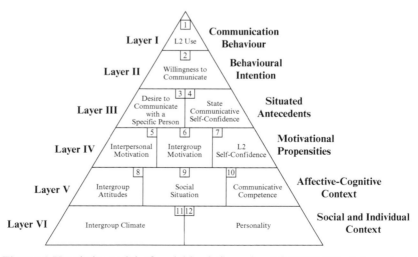

Figure 1 Heuristic model of variables influencing L2 WTC (MacIntyre et al., 1998, p. 547, reproduced by permission of John Wiley & Sons, Inc.)

while the latter involves learners' self-assessment of their L2 skills and anxiety provoked when using the L2. Importantly, L2 self-confidence is treated as a trait in comparison to its state counterpart, state communicative self-confidence (Box 4) situated in Layer III. Layer III comprises situated antecedents of WTC, meaning that their influences on WTC are transient. Another of such antecedent is the desire to communicate (DC) with a specific person (Box 3), which depends on individuals' affiliation motives and control motives during interactions with particular interlocutors. The distal and proximal antecedents together culminate in the state of WTC, which in turn directly predicts L2 use. Hence, WTC is considered the final stage before overt engagement in communication (MacIntyre et al., 2001).

This pyramid model, as noted by MacIntyre (2020), was proposed ten years ahead of the advancement of the CDST articulated in Larsen-Freeman and Cameron's (2008) work. The CDST is considered a significant theoretical enhancement to WTC theory and research. It offers a valuable framework for understanding the fluctuating nature of WTC across both longer-term and shorter-term timescales, attributing these changes to the interaction of various processes. Reexamining the pyramid model, MacIntyre (2020) noted that while the model acknowledges the situated nature of WTC, it makes no mention of the timescales over which WTC fluctuates or the measurement of state WTC. Furthermore, the model does not address how multilayered processes it incorporates interact across various timescales. Adopting the lens of the CDST, MacIntyre and Legatto (2011) made pioneering efforts to examine the dynamic fluctuations of WTC, which signified a "dynamic turn" in WTC research.

Extending on MacIntyre's (2020) new theoretical insights, the seminal WTC model (MacIntyre et al., 1998) has been recently expanded into a three-dimensional (3D) model (Henry & MacIntyre, 2024) based on Henry and their colleagues' innovative research into WTC in multilingual contexts (e.g., Henry et al., 2021a, 2021b). Arising from the research conducted in the Swedish context where L2 English and L3 Swedish are viable media of communication, the 3D model of WTC (see Figure 2) schematizes the multifaceted and fluid interactions of the constituent elements included in the original WTC model to provide a holistic understanding of WTC in multilingual scenarios. As elucidated by Henry and MacIntyre (2024), the original two-dimensional (2D) model outlines two primary pathways for the emergence of WTC: the LEFT-side pathway, which emphasizes intergroup-related factors and the DC with specific individuals, and the RIGHT-side pathway that focuses on individual factors and confidence levels. Moving up these pathways illuminates how factors at lower levels feed into factors at upper levels in communication situations using *one* L2. The 3D model tailors to situations where more than one L2 can be used,

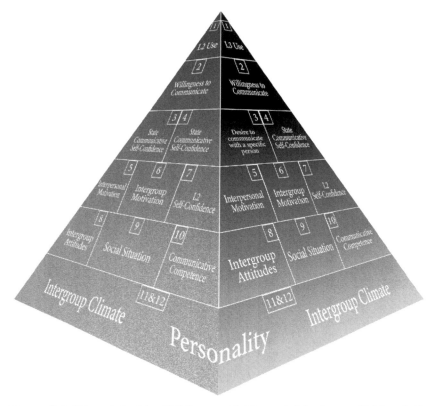

Figure 2 A 3D model of the WTC pyramid (Henry & MacIntyre, 2024, p. 262, reproduced by permission of Multilingual Matters)

depicted by two interconnected lateral surfaces, each being a mirror of the original 2D model. As shown in Figure 2, the two interconnected lateral surfaces start with a homogenous foundation and progressively transit upward in shading or hue, culminating in a pronounced differentiation at its zenith. Such a gradation exemplifies the nuanced progression of WTC, particularly in environments conducive to code-switching, where distal factors largely retain their stability, yet those within the pyramid's upper echelons exhibit elevated variability upon linguistic shifts.

More importantly, this 3D model underscores the inherently dynamic nature of WTC in multilingual communication situations. Henry and MacIntyre (2024) argued that in multilingual scenarios, where multiple languages might be in play, the LEFT-side and RIGHT-side pathways are not sufficient for accounting for the increased communication complexity. Hence, to replace the simpler "pathways" of the 2D model, they proposed the concept of "corridors" as located within the 3D model, which connects the factors in the L2 and L3 surfaces. These corridors signify the intricate dynamics of multilingual communication, especially in situations where code-switching is prominent.

In brief, while the L2 heuristic model (MacIntyre et al., 1998) deviated from the trait-like approach to WTC in L1 communication research (McCroskey & Richmond, 1991) by accentuating the situational characteristics of WTC in L2, capricious interactions between various factors or forces in local educational or communication contexts depicted in numerous subsequent studies have called for "a different theoretical starting point" (Henry & MacIntyre, 2024, p. 17). About a decade later, subscribing to the CDST, MacIntyre and Legatto (2011) conceptualized WTC as a dynamic system. This dynamic perspective has further motivated researchers to explore even more intricate interactions of various processes and the fluctuations of WTC embedded in plurilingual situations. Hence, the original pyramid WTC model is expanded into the 3D model to accommodate increasingly multilingual and multicultural communicative encounters.

The foregoing review has mainly focused on seminal and novel conceptualizations of WTC in the L2 field over more than two decades. The next section will detail diverse perspectives that have informed research on WTC.

3 Various Perspectives on Researching WTC

In this section, various perspectives for approaching WTC are presented, supplemented by pertinent sample studies. While there may be minor overlap with the subsequent section, as some empirical WTC studies are relevant to both, each section has a distinct focus: this one on varied research perspectives, and the next on the detailed factors associated with WTC. In addition, it is important to note that the terminology used to describe these perspectives is applied in a broad sense, aiming to present a clear and logical depiction of the research landscape, rather than to assert any official definitions.

3.1 A Social Psychological Perspective

Initial research on WTC (e.g., MacIntyre et al., 2002; MacIntyre & Blackie, 2012; MacIntyre & Charos, 1996; Yashima, 2002) can be viewed to predominantly adopt a social psychological perspective. This approach is evident in the heuristic model (MacIntyre et al., 1998), which upon careful analysis, embodies concepts central to Gardner's (1985) socio-educational model, such as integrativeness, attitudes towards the learning situation, and motivation. Within Gardner's (1985) model, integrativeness stands out as a key concept, denoting learners' genuine interest in learning the L2 to connect with the L2 community, which are fostered by positive attitudes towards that community. Originating in the context of Canadian bilingualism – where Anglophone and Francophone communities coexist – Gardner's (1985) framework emphasizes the significance of intergroup attitudes, such as control or affiliation, as important social psychological factors driving learners' motivation to learn the L2. Hence, in MacIntyre et al.'s (1998) model, intergroup climate, intergroup attitudes, and intergroup motivation are treated as important social, affective, and motivational variables influencing WTC.

In addition, early WTC studies (Baker & MacIntyre, 2000; MacIntyre et al., 2002, 2003) adopting this perspective often operationalized attitudes (i.e., integrativeness and attitudes toward the learning situation) and motivation by using scale items from Gardner and MacIntyre's (1993) widely adopted Attitude/Motivation Test Battery. For instance, Baker and MacIntyre (2000) used 11 items from Gardner and MacIntyre (1993) to measure Anglophone students' attitudes and motivation to learn French. However, arguing that integrativeness may not be necessarily present in Japanese learners who learn English as a foreign language (EFL) and view English as connected to the global community rather than a specific target community, Yashima (2002) proposed an alternative attitudinal concept, namely international posture. International posture refers to learners' interest in international affairs, willingness to study or work abroad, and readiness to engage in intercultural communication. In short, this construct reflects EFL learners' openness to different cultures. International posture was operationalized by four aspects: intercultural friendship orientation, interest in international vocation/activities, interest in foreign affairs, and intergroup approach-avoidance tendency (Yashima, 2002). It has been validated as a pertinent attitudinal variable in other contexts such as Iran (Ghonsooly et al., 2012; Khajavy et al., 2016).

Although WTC studies adopting a social psychological perspective have focused on diverse attitudinal constructs, they have commonly explored learners' psychological tendencies to use the L2 within a broad social or even imagined international context. These studies, typically employing quantitative methodologies, have provided relatively comprehensive evidence of how WTC is the function of an interplay between individual psychological factors and wider social contextual influences. However, this perspective is insufficient to capture the finer nuances of learners' WTC in specific microlevel classroom contexts, or to track its evolution across these settings.

3.2 A Cultural Perspective

WTC is a particularly important concept in EFL contexts, where English serves as a high-stakes academic subject crucial for learners' education. Therefore, understanding EFL learners' WTC requires considering both the culture of communication and the culture of learning in the local context. In this regard, Wen and Clément (2003) explored the potential influences of Chinese culture, rooted in Confucianism, on Chinese students' unwillingness to communicate in the EFL classroom. They highlighted characteristics such as an other-directed self and a submissive learning style prevalent among Chinese students, which may impact students' WTC. The former concept suggests that students' self-perception and behavior are significantly influenced by others, while the latter indicates students' submission to teachers' authoritative role in the Chinese culture of learning. These cultural factors may contribute to students' reluctance to speak up in English, driven by a fear of losing face or habitual comfort with teacher-centered teaching approaches.

Arguing that MacIntyre et al.'s (1998) model primarily reflects Western-based research, Wen and Clément (2003) proposed a revised WTC model in the Chinese EFL classroom. In this model, a distinction is made between the desire to communicate (DC) and WTC. They described a desire as reflecting "a deliberate choice or preference" (Wen & Clément, 2003, p. 25) whereas willingness signals the readiness for action. The DC and WTC are placed on two ends of a unidirectional arrow, between which four clusters of factors are posited to influence the extent to which Chinese EFL students' DC develops into WTC. These clusters include: societal context (i.e., group cohesiveness, teacher support), personal factors (i.e., risk-taking, tolerance of ambiguity), motivational orientation (i.e., affiliation, task-orientation), and affective perceptions (i.e., inhibited monitor, positive expectation of evaluation). According to Wen and Clément (2003), although Chinese learners may have the preference for speaking up, such a desire may be mediated by the complex interaction between the aforementioned factors.

This cultural perspective can find echoes in the literature that documented cultural influences on interpersonal communication and in perceptions of learning. For instance, it was reported that Chinese people value the trait of being modest instead of assertive, and out of concerns for face, silence may be adopted as a face-saving strategy (Liu, 2002). In educational contexts, particularly within the Chinese culture of learning, being disciplined and attentive is often prioritized over being talkative. This preference is succinctly expressed in the distinction articulated by Hu (2002), where Chinese students are expected to be "mentally active" rather than "verbally active" (p. 100). It seems legitimate to propose that the Chinese culture of learning may function as "the hidden curriculum" (Cortazzi & Jin, 1996, p. 169) that subtly influences the dynamics of teaching and learning processes.

Several studies on WTC have provided evidence for discussing WTC through a cultural lens. Peng's (2007) study identified such cultural influences on Chinese university students' WTC in class. In her study, some students expressed their concerns about being laughed at or being viewed as showing off, while some other students reported that they were not accustomed to communicating ideas in class. Coincidently, such cultural influence was pronounced by a group of teachers in Wei and Cao's (2021) study. The teachers in this study pointed out that some students might avoid speaking up for the purpose of not appearing assertive or showing off. Yue's (2014) case study on Chinese EFL university students also reported that students' WTC was influenced by an insider orientation, a feeling of belonging to a group that is intimately connected to the collectivist nature of the Chinese culture (Wen & Clément, 2003). Similarly, Lee et al. (2021) conducted a cross-cultural study comparing WTC among Korean and Swedish students. Their results showed that Korean students who learned English primarily to meet others' expectations (a high level of ought-to L2 self) were more likely to initiate communication, a tendency not observed in their Swedish counterparts. However, it should be noted that while culture may play a significant role in shaping WTC or unwillingness to communicate, it should not be seen as a panacea for universal explanations. Ushioda (2009) cautioned against using culture to make "broad brushstrokes only" (p. 218), as this approach can lead to overlooking individual variations. Nevertheless, the impact of specific Indigenous cultures is undeniably profound, forming a foundational backdrop against which individuals' WTC and communication behaviors are developed.

3.3 A Dynamic Perspective

The conceptualization of WTC as a dynamic system, as proposed by MacIntyre and Legatto (2011), has paved the way for a dynamic perspective in WTC research. Dynamic systems are characterized by several properties: they consist of interrelated components, are in a state of constant change, and self-organize into either repeller states (unstable states prone to change from slight perturbation) or attractor states (stable states that dynamic system settles into overtime; Hiver, 2015; Larsen-Freeman & Cameron, 2008). Embracing this perspective, MacIntyre and Legatto (2011) conceptualized WTC as a dynamic system subject to continuous transformation due to the interaction of multiple factors across different timescales. To capture these momentary changes in WTC,

MacIntyre and Legatto (2011) developed the idiodynamic method. This method requires L2 learners to watch recordings of themselves performing communicative tasks in the L2 and rate their WTC at momentary intervals (details are presented in Section 5.3). The findings revealed that WTC exhibited the characteristics of a dynamic system, and contrary to the negative relationship commonly identified through quantitative methods, anxiety and WTC were found to evince nonlinear and complex relationships (positive, negative, or independent) at different time points.

This dynamic perspective of WTC has inspired many subsequent studies in laboratory-like settings (Nematizadeh & Wood, 2019; Pawlak & Mystkowska-Wiertelak, 2015; Wood, 2016) and in online synchronous group discussions (Nematizadeh & Cao, 2023). For instance, Wood (2016) investigated the relationship between WTC and speech fluency of four Japanese L1 learners of EFL. The participants were asked to perform a picture description task with a native English speaker. Employing a similar idiodynamic method to that of MacIntyre and Legatto (2011), Wood (2016) observed complex dynamic relations between WTC and fluency, which were influenced by various cognitive (e.g., vocabulary retrieval) and affective factors (e.g., sense of frustration). Extending this approach to an online synchronous context, Nematizadeh and Cao (2023) involved seven Farsi-speaking ESL speakers in six discussion tasks conducted via Zoom, each moderated by different facilitators. Similarly, the participants rated their WTC levels on a scale between −5 and +5 at five-minute intervals, prompted by a beeping sound. Their study identified complex interactions between many internal and external forces, with some influences similar to those found in previous studies (e.g., topics or questions under discussion) and others unique to the online environment (e.g., technical issues or distractions from background noise caused by other participants' microphones).

This dynamic perspective has also informed much research conducted in language classroom settings. Contrasting with the laboratory-based tracking of WTC in MacIntyre and Legatto's (2011) study, the dynamic fluctuations of classroom WTC were traced using a method analogous to the idiodynamic method, which is termed "the spaced-interval timing technique" by Ducker (2022, p. 222). For instance, Pawlak and colleagues (Mystkowska-Wiertelak & Pawlak, 2017; Pawlak et al., 2016) tracked the dynamic changes of WTC by asking students to rate their WTC (ranging between −10 and +10) on a grid at five-minute intervals during class sessions, which was regularly prompted by a prerecorded beep. In a parallel vein, Ducker (2022) utilized video recordings of students in conversation-oriented classroom activities. The recordings were subsequently used in stimulated recall interviews, where students self-assessed their WTC. Their studies support that WTC dynamically changes in the timeframe of a classroom context, and multiple factors such as interests in and knowledge about topics or rapport with interlocutors contribute to variations in WTC across groups and individuals.

Applying the principles of CDST, Peng (2020b) examined how WTC and silence, as two dynamic systems, fluctuated in three class sessions, each lasting 90 minutes, over one semester. In particular, she aimed to explore how WTC and silence interacted to induce "variation, non-linearity and different attractor states" of four focal students' communication behavior (Peng, 2020b, p. 147). She identified mainly five predominant attractor states among the focal students: *unwilling and silent* (i.e., being unready and unwilling to talk, and voluntarily silent), *capable but silent* (i.e., being ready but voluntarily silent), *desirous but silent* (i.e., being desirous to talk but unready, and hence silent), *silent yet yearning* (i.e., being silent but ready and yearning to be nominated), and *willing and breaking silence* (i.e., WTC surpassing silence). The study revealed that *unwilling and silent* and *capable but silent* were more commonly observed and exhibited greater persistence. She thus postulated that when students' communication behavior settled down on the first two attractor states, it would require greater force to trigger changes.

Peng's (2020b) findings were to some extent corroborated by Wei and Cao's (2021) study. Focusing on English for Academic Purposes (EAP) classrooms, their study sought to understand the perspectives of both teachers and students regarding student participation. Three types of participation were identified: willing, silent, and forced. Willing participation was characterized by voluntary engagement in class activities and discussions. In contrast, silent participation was observed among students who, despite their lack of verbal contributions, demonstrated comprehension and engagement. Forced participation typically involved specific students and was initiated by the teacher. Wei and Cao (2021) emphasized the importance of recognizing silent participation as a legitimate form of engagement in specific cultures where the roles of teachers and students are traditionally viewed, respectively, as knowledge givers and receivers.

In a similar effort to build on the concepts in CDST, Zhou (2023b) tracked the experience of six multilingual and multicultural students in a Chinese as a foreign language classroom. This study aimed to discern how the students' WTC translated into talk using the L2. By collating and analyzing various data collected through classroom observations, learner journals, video-stimulated recall interviews, and semi-structured interviews, she identified thirteen learner-internal and learner-external factors that interacted to form various interactional patterns, based on which the learners' WTC self-organized into different attractor states (pro-talk vs. against-talk). Zhou's (2023a) study further illuminated the intricate and often covert interplay of multiple determinants impacting the realization of WTC into actual talk, which is dynamic, nonlinear, self-organizing, and co-adaptive. Overall, the "dynamic turn" in WTC research has contributed to an in-depth understanding of the complex and ever-changing dynamics of L2 learners' WTC, which reinforces the need for educators to adapt pedagogical practices to address these properties to promote learners' WTC and participation.

3.4 An Ecological Perspective

Research into WTC has been informed by an ecological perspective that views individual learners as embedded within, influenced by, but simultaneously influencing their broader contextual environments. Ecology is defined as the "study of the relationships between all the various organisms and their physical environment" (van Lier, 2002, p. 144). This perspective on language learning prioritizes the centrality of the reciprocity between individuals and the surrounding environment. Second language learners' WTC is perceived as co-constructed and dynamically changing, which is shaped by the interplay of various individual and environmental factors (Cao, 2011). The WTC studies framed from the ecological perspective were often conducted in L2 classroom settings, which provide detailed insights into how WTC is situated and changes within various levels of contexts.

Cao (2011) adopted an ecological perspective in a multiple case study to examine the dynamic and situated nature of WTC in an L2 class in New Zealand. During a three-week pilot study and a twenty-week main study, data were collected through classroom observations, stimulated recall interviews, and students' reflective journals. Cao (2011) concluded that situational WTC dynamically emerged from the interaction between a multitude of individual characteristics (e.g., self-confidence, perceived opportunity to communicate), classroom environmental conditions (e.g., topic, teacher), and linguistic factors (e.g., L2 proficiency, reliance on L1). Cao's (2011) study demonstrates the practical application of an ecological perspective on WTC in L2 classrooms.

Peng (2012) applied Bronfenbrenner's (1979, 1993) ecosystems model to investigate Chinese EFL students' WTC as embedded in various layers of settings: microsystem, mesosystem, exosystem, and macrosystem (see also Peng, 2014). These ecosystems are often depicted as concentric circles, with the microsystem at the core. In Peng's (2012) study, these settings refer to, respectively, the EFL classroom, the connections between the classroom and other settings containing the students (e.g., students' past experience), the connections between the classroom and other settings, at least one of which does not contain the students, and the overarching educational and sociocultural context. Peng's (2012) findings led to an ecological interpretation of WTC in

EFL classrooms, conceptualized as being "socioculturally constructed as a function of the interaction of individual and environmental factors" (p. 203) which extends beyond the classroom walls.

The adoption of an ecological perspective in WTC research has foregrounded the interconnectedness and interdependence of various factors often examined in isolation. While not all subsequent studies have explicitly utilized Bronfenbrenner's (1979, 1993) framework, the tenets of an ecological perspective have motivated researchers to focus on classroom environment (Khajavy et al., 2016; Peng & Woodrow, 2010) or classroom social climate (Joe et al., 2017) in relation to WTC. This line of research is particularly relevant in EFL contexts, where the L2 classroom often serves as the primary platform for students to practice their L2 use.

3.5 A Multimodal Perspective

Another notable avenue in WTC research is the examination of the relationship of WTC with multimodal affordances (Peng, 2019a, 2019b; Peng et al., 2017), which represents a multimodal perspective. This perspective recognizes the significance of various communicative modes beyond language, such as visual images, gestures, and facial expressions. These are often referred to as semiotic resources (O'Halloran, 2005) or modes (Kress, 2010). Collectively, these multi-semiotic and multimodal resources can be termed as multimodality (Peng, 2019a). Kessler (2022) defined multimodality as "an individual's use of different *modes* (i.e. channels of communication) for the purpose of conveying meaning" (p. 551; italics in the original).

The role of multimodality in L2 learning and teaching has been extensively explored. Example areas of study are vocabulary learning (Bisson et al., 2014; Lin et al., 2022), multimodal composing (see Yi et al., 2020), and broader areas in language teaching (Lim, 2021; Morell, 2018). For instance, Bisson et al.'s (2014) study detected a significant effect of repeated exposure to multimodal stimuli on the incidental acquisition of Welsh vocabulary among native English speakers. Lim (2021) provided book-length descriptions of how teachers used gestures, movements, spaces, and other tools, together with language, to convey meanings in classrooms. He posited the concept of "embodied teaching," which refers to teachers' application of their knowledge to their teaching practice, which is crucial in shaping students' learning experience. As Lim (2021) emphasized, "[w]hether the students feel safe to participate or are inhibited from speaking up are often a result of the meanings they perceive from their teachers' embodied semiosis" (p. 2). These insights align well with the adoption of a multimodal perspective in WTC research.

WTC research from a multimodal perspective has mainly adopted systemic functional multimodal discourse analysis (SF-MDA), an approach rooted in Halliday's (1978) systemic functional linguistics (SFL). Systemic functional linguistics views language as a social semiotic for meaning-making, focusing on the analysis of three metafunctions in meaning-making: ideational, interpersonal, and textual. The ideational function is concerned with representing experience, interpersonal function focuses on maintaining interactions, and textual function pertains to textual organization and structure. The SF-MDA expands upon the SFL framework to consider not only linguistic but also other semiotic resources and analyzes how different modes (e.g., language, images, and gestures) collaboratively contribute to meaning-making in a discourse.

Kress and van Leeuwen (2006) adopted Halliday's (1978) three metafunctions of language to analyze visual representations, viewing them as integral semiotic resources in the construction of meaning. In line with Halliday's (1978) framework, they proposed three types of meaning encoded in visual images: representational, interactive, and compositional. Representational meaning is concerned with how objects and their relations are represented in visual images; interactive meaning is the representation of the relationship between the producer and the receiver of a visual image; and compositional meaning derives from the arrangement and organization of elements in visual images. Furthermore, Halliday's (1978) framework has been extended to analyze other semiotics such as gestures (see Hood, 2011; Lim, 2021), thus broadening the applicability of SFL principles in the multimodal analysis of communication.

WTC research adopting a multimodal perspective has been mainly initiated by Peng and colleagues (Peng, 2019a, 2019b; Peng et al., 2017). Adopting SF-MDA, Peng et al. (2017) analyzed language teachers' use of semiotic resources in terms of language, gestures, and gaze within two distinct classroom scenarios captured on video. The two scenarios were characterized by differing levels of WTC, hence labeled as high-WTC and low-WTC scenarios, according to the self-ratings of four focal students. The discourse semantic features of the two scenarios were also analyzed and compared (a detailed account is presented in Section 5.4.1).

In another study, Peng (2019b) focused on four students in a classroom setting that was observed and video-documented across one semester. This study entailed an analysis of interactive meanings instantiated in two visual images in the teacher's PowerPoint slides based on Kress and van Leeuwen's (2006) framework. These visuals were identified to most trigger the focal students' WTC inside the class. The study found a correlation between thoughtfully designed multimodal PowerPoint slides alongside multimodal resources such as gestures, facial expressions, and voice, and the students' WTC, as reflected in their retrospections during stimulated recall interviews.

Peng (2019a) further explored the relationships between Chinese EFL university students' perceived multimodal pedagogic effects, classroom environment, and WTC in English by employing structural equation modeling (SEM). The results showed that teachers' effective use of audio/video and their gestures and spatial position were direct predictors of WTC, while teachers' voices/facial expressions indirectly predicted WTC. This study marks the first attempt to operationalize the perceived effects of multimodal pedagogies and quantitatively explore how these perceived effects were related to WTC. Overall, multimodal affordances constitute important resources for meaning-making in L2 classrooms. Peng (2021) proposed that WTC can be viewed as being embedded in classroom multimodal affordances, to which its individual and contextual antecedents are inherently tied. This proposition is schematized in Figure 3.

Before concluding this section, it is important to note the limited evidence regarding the role of multimodality in L2 learners' WTC. Employing SF-MDA requires researchers to be equipped with knowledge and analytic skills in

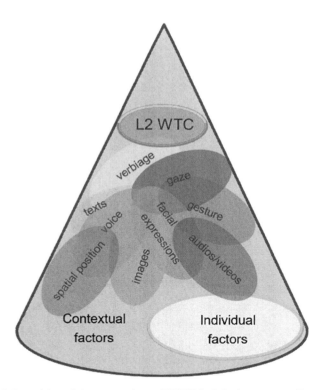

Figure 3 A multimodal perspective of WTC in L2 classrooms (Peng, 2021)

theoretical linguistics such as SFL (Halliday, 1978). However, it seems that researchers from the realms of theoretical linguistics and applied linguistics are on two parallel tracks whose paths have seldom crossed. Certainly, no clear boundaries exist between the two realms (Malmkjær, 2010). In WTC research, empirical evidence gathered from L2 learners can provide the "reception perspective" often absent in SF-MDA studies (Holsanova, 2012, p. 252), and the analysis of multimodal affordances informed by SF-MDA can increase the explanatory power of multimodal classroom discourse in understanding learners' WTC (Peng, 2019b). Furthermore, integrating detailed analysis of classroom discourse adds an important cognitive dimension to WTC research, as echoed by the growing emphasis on analyzing learners' output (Ducker, 2022; Zhou, 2023a, 2023b) and teacher discourse (Yang & Yin, 2022). Therefore, WTC research can benefit from interdisciplinary perspectives and approaches to move beyond its heavy reliance on learners' self-reported psychological experiences. In brief, multimodality has undeniably featured modern language classrooms. As Kessler (2022) rightly pointed out, current digital technologies have resulted in the fact that "multimodality now permeates numerous facets of teachers' everyday practices" (p. 551). This proposition also ties into the digital perspective on WTC research discussed in the next section.

3.6 A Digital Perspective

In this section, the delineation of a digital perspective aims to emphasize L2 communication situations shaped by contemporary technological and social media advancements that may impact L2 learners' WTC. It is not suggested that this digital perspective is mutually exclusive from the multimodal perspective previously presented since human communication is inherently multimodal (O'Halloran, 2011). Hence, a digital perspective is used here to accentuate an explicit focus on digital contexts or technology-mediated communication contexts.

Lee and colleagues are representative researchers who have examined L2 learners' WTC in digital contexts (Lee & Drajati, 2020; Lee & Hsieh, 2019; Lee & Lee, 2020a). Lee and Drajati (2020) validated an 11-item measuring three factors of WTC: WTC inside the classroom, L2 WTC outside the classroom, and WTC in the context of informal digital learning of English (IDLE). They also explored the relationships between affective factors and WTC in the three settings. Lee and Hsieh (2019) found that among EFL undergraduate students in Taiwan, high levels of grit and L2 confidence were associated with high levels of WTC in the three settings, while L2 anxiety showed no significant correlation with WTC in digital settings. They indicated that digital contexts may provide social support and alleviate students' anxiety in communication. In another study, Lee and Lee (2020a) observed that younger learners with high L2 self-confidence and more frequent exposure to virtual intercultural experiences had higher L2 WTC in digital settings. These studies have pointed to the significant potential of digital settings in fostering L2 learners' WTC and L2 use, particularly among tech-savvy younger generations (Bennett, 2012).

Of note, while most of the previously mentioned studies have utilized cross-sectional designs, Taherian et al. (2023) adopted a longitudinal approach to investigate the extent to which foreign language boredom mediated the relationship between IDLE and WTC. This study collected data in four waves over four months from 354 Iranian university learners, using scale items to measure the variables in question. The results indicated that at the intraindividual level, learners with initially low scores on IDLE and WTC exhibited greater variability in these areas, whereas those with low initial scores on boredom experienced less changes in boredom. At the interindividual level, significant positive growth in IDLE and WTC and significant negative growth in boredom were observed. In addition, boredom was a significant mediator in the long-term relationship between IDLE and WTC.

Departing from the aforementioned survey-based studies, researchers have taken advantage of technologies and explored how WTC may be promoted by means of technology-mediated communication. In a study by Reinders and Wattana (2015), thirty Thai EFL university students engaged in a digital game-based learning mode over fifteen weeks. Interviews with five of these students showed that gameplay could increase their WTC. In addition, digital storytelling (DST) has emerged as a promising tool (Shen et al., 2024). Defined as a multimodal practice that "uses new media technology to produce short, personal narratives using high-quality sound and image" (Vinogradova et al., 2011, p. 175), DST has been gaining traction in L2 classrooms (see Shen et al., 2024). Shen et al.'s (2022) study involved a DST workshop for sixty-nine undergraduate students in China. The workshop participants completed stages of prescript writing, video making, postscript writing, and sharing their DST videos in an online premiere. Twenty-two of the students participated in semi-structured post-project interviews. This study found that the participants' WTC in writing was significantly higher when composing the postscripts compared to the prescripts. This finding aligns with Luan et al.'s (2023) quasi-experiment conducted during the COVID-19 pandemic. During sixteen weeks in a college English course, a DST-based online flipped learning approach was implemented in the experimental class while an online flipped learning approach was used in the comparison class. The results showed that the experimental class scored significantly higher on the WTC measure than the comparison class and such difference was supported by their interview data. However, Huang's (2023) quasi-experimental study involving two DST tasks in the experimental class found a positive but not significant impact on WTC. Given the scarcity of research in this area, further empirical investigation is necessary to pin down the role of DST in generating L2 learners' WTC.

Another innovative attempt is to explore whether L2 learners' WTC is malleable in L2 communication mediated by robots and other intelligent personal assistants (IPAs; Hsieh et al., 2023; Tai, 2024; Tai & Chen, 2023). Hsieh et al. (2023) developed a robot and tangible objects (R&T) learning system that consisted of a robot, a tablet, a cellphone, and other tangible objects which aimed to maximize students' experiences of physically interacting with the system. Utilizing this system, twenty-nine elementary students in Taiwan engaged in location-specific tasks in English with the R&T system for five consecutive days. The outcomes indicated the students' significant improvement in pronunciation and WTC. That said, a more robust conclusion could have been reached if the experiment had been conducted over a longer period.

Further creative studies have examined the potential influences of AI-supported interactions on learners' WTC. Tai and Chen (2023) employed Google Assistant, an intelligent personal assistant (IPA), in language learning activities with eighth-grade EFL learners for two weeks. It was found that Google Assistant significantly enhanced the students' WTC and communicative confidence while reducing their anxiety. Such influences of IPA-assisted interactions on WTC were further confirmed in Tai's (2024) experimental study with three groups, a total of ninety-two first-year college students. The students were invited to participate in interactive out-of-class activities for twelve weeks. The IPA group who had interacted with Alexa or Google Assistant through a smartphone showed significantly higher WTC compared to groups interacting with L1 and L2 English speakers. Zhang et al.'s (2024) recent six-week quasi-experimental study also confirmed that employing Lora, an AI-speaking assistant, significantly boosted WTC among sixty-five Chinese EFL students in the experimental group of the study. These innovative studies underscore the promising role of AI-assisted tools in augmenting L2 learners' WTC. This aligns with the emerging myriad of possibilities in language education enabled by AI-assisted apps or large language models (Jeon et al., 2023; Liang et al., 2021; Lin et al., 2022; Liu & Ma, 2023).

4 Key Factors Associated with WTC

WTC is a multifaceted concept intricately linked with various psychological, social, and linguistic factors commonly discussed in SLA, as encapsulated in MacIntyre et al.'s (1998) heuristic model. In this section, major factors internal and external to L2 learners that have been empirically found to be associated with WTC are first presented, followed by a review of linguistic and nonlinguistic outcomes associated with WTC.

4.1 Individual Attributes Associated with L2 WTC

Amidst a myriad of individual factors that may account for WTC, language anxiety, perceived communicative competence, L2 confidence, attitudes, and motivation can be viewed as a cluster widely acknowledged in many WTC studies (Liu & Jackson, 2008; MacIntyre et al., 2002, 2003). Language anxiety and perceived communicative competence are established antecedents of WTC in L2 contexts (MacIntyre et al., 2003; MacIntyre & Charos, 1996). These two concepts were often collapsed to form a higher-level concept, namely L2 self-confidence, which has also been shown to directly predict WTC (Ghonsooly et al., 2012; Lin, 2019; Peng & Woodrow, 2010; Yashima, 2002). Hence, it is widely recognized that learners with higher perceived competence and lower anxiety levels are more inclined to engage in L2 communication. More importantly, it is believed that learners' self-perceptions of competence play a more important role in WTC than their actual level of competence (Baker & MacIntyre, 2000; MacIntyre et al., 2003), especially in cases where anxious learners are prone to underestimating their actual linguistic abilities (MacIntyre et al., 1997). Evidence from social network analysis confirmed that WTC was predicted by learners' self-rated L2 proficiency (Gallagher, 2019). The concepts of integrativeness and motivation central to Gardner's (1985) socio-educational model have been found to correlate positively with WTC among English L1 students learning French L2 (Baker & MacIntyre, 2000; MacIntyre et al., 2002, 2003). Furthermore, international posture as an alternative attitudinal factor was also found to directly predict WTC, while the impact of motivation on WTC was indirect and routed through L2 communication confidence (Yashima, 2002; Yashima et al., 2004).

Motivation, albeit with various conceptualizations, has been consistently found to be associated with WTC. Besides Gardner's (1985) conceptualization, intrinsic motivation, and extrinsic motivation from the self-determination theory (SDT) proposed by Deci and Ryan (1985) have been incorporated into WTC research. Intrinsic motivation refers to individuals' engagement in an activity out of genuine interest or for its inherent satisfaction and enjoyment, while extrinsic motivation pertains to individuals' engagement in an activity for external rewards or pressures. It has been found that WTC is indirectly predicted by SDT-based motivation (Khajavy et al., 2016; Lin, 2019; Peng & Woodrow, 2010) or directly predicted by identified regulation, a form of extrinsic motivation (Joe et al., 2017). Recent research has also explored the relationship between WTC and the L2 motivational self system, the reconceptualization of motivation from the future self-perspective proposed by Dörnyei (2005). The ideal L2 self, reflecting learners' vision of themselves as effective L2 users in the future, was shown to be a significant predictor of L2 WTC (Lan et al., 2021; Lee & Lee, 2020b; Lee & Lu, 2023; Teimouri, 2017; Zhang et al., 2022). The ought-to L2 self, defined as the attributes that learners feel obligatory to possess to meet external expectations or to avoid negative outcomes, alongside the ideal L2 self, have also been found to indirectly predict WTC in a positive and negative manner, respectively (Peng, 2015). Taken together, these findings illuminate the important role of motivation in energizing L2 learners' proclivity to use the L2.

The rise of positive psychology in SLA (MacIntyre et al., 2016) in recent years has led to the addition of more individual attributes to the spectrum of WTC research, such as enjoyment and grit. Foreign language enjoyment is a positive emotion generated when one's skills are aligned with challenges, and thereby their psychological needs are satisfied (Dewaele & MacIntyre, 2014). This enjoyment may be intrinsically linked to the satisfaction of one of the three fundamental psychological needs, namely, the need for competence (Deci & Ryan, 1985). Along with autonomy and relatedness, competence constitutes the triad of core psychological needs of human beings (Deci & Ryan, 1985). Foreign language enjoyment is often contrasted with its well-established emotional negative counterpart, foreign language anxiety in WTC research. Pertinent research has shown that enjoyment is a significant predictor of WTC, and it exerts a stronger impact on WTC than does foreign language anxiety (Feng et al., 2023; Khajavy et al., 2018; Lee, Xie et al., 2021; Li et al., 2022). Besides, recent research has demonstrated direct correlations between WTC and factors like boredom (Fattahi et al., 2023; Li et al., 2022; Zhang et al., 2022) and grit (Lan et al., 2021; Lee & Hsieh, 2019; Lee & Lee, 2020a). These varying relationships between WTC and other factors might stem from researchers' initial hypotheses that resulted in different model specifications. It is important to acknowledge that the predominance of cross-sectional, self-reported data in many of these studies suggests that the associations between WTC and these variables could be at best interpreted as correlational rather than causal.

Learner beliefs, which are inherently related to WTC (Dörnyei, 2005), often have a less immediate but more enduring impact on WTC. These beliefs may often elude learners' conscious awareness while subtly influencing their WTC. Peng (2014) identified learner beliefs as distal factors, and learners' beliefs about English learning and beliefs about classroom communication behavior indirectly influenced WTC. Similarly, Fushino (2010) also posited that learners' beliefs about L2 group work, such as the usefulness and value of group work, indirectly influenced WTC via communicative confidence in L2 group work, a hypothesis supported by SEM results. Zhong (2013) in a multiple case study found that learners' beliefs about collaborative learning and beliefs about what constitute sources for learning (peers vs. experts or teachers) shaped their WTC and oral participation in collaborative learning activities. More recently, language mindset, a concept related to learner beliefs, has been explored. Language mindset refers to learners' underlying beliefs about the plasticity or rigidity of their capacity to learn languages (Lou & Noels, 2019). Dweck's (1999) typology suggests that language learners with a fixed mindset tend to view their capacity to learn a language as static and immutable, whereas those with a growth mindset view their capacity as malleable and subject to enhancement through deliberate exertion and sustained efforts. Language growth mindset was found to indirectly predict WTC through its effects on boredom (Zhang et al., 2022) or perceived communicative competence (Zarrinabadi et al., 2021). In Hejazi et al.'s (2023) study among 551 Iranian students, learners' growth language mindset moderated the relationships between teacher support and WTC and between L2 anxiety and WTC.

Personality represents factors with more enduring influences on WTC. It has often been approached from Goldberg's (2012) "The Big Five" traits (i.e., openness to experience, conscientiousness, extraversion, agreeableness, and neuroticism), but various findings have been reported. Zhang (2020) discovered a correlation between state WTC and all five personality traits, whereas trait WTC was significantly related to openness to experience, conscientiousness, and agreeableness. Two of the "Big Five," openness to experience and extraversion, were found to significantly predict WTC (Fatima et al., 2020). Other studies identified indirect effects of openness to experience (a.k.a. intellect) and extraversion on WTC (Ghonsooly et al., 2012; MacIntyre & Charos, 1996), while agreeableness directly influenced WTC (MacIntyre & Charos, 1996). In addition, Lin (2019) further delineated the indirect pathway from the "Big Five" traits to WTC (i.e., personality → international posture → motivation → self-perceived communication competence → WTC), which were confirmed through SEM. Overall, agreeableness seems to be the most consistent predictor of WTC.

Finally, demographic factors such as gender and age are viewed to be associated with WTC, although inconsistent and relatively scant evidence has been reported. For instance, no significant gender effect on WTC was found in Baker and MacIntyre's (2000) study among students from Grades 10, 11, and 12, and Tavakoli and Davoudi's (2017) study among Iranian EFL learners aged between 11 and 50. However, other studies reported that for junior high school students, girls tended to have higher WTC than boys (Donovan & MacIntyre, 2004; MacIntyre et al., 2002), while students in Grades 8 and 9 had higher WTC than those in Grade 7 (MacIntyre et al., 2002). A survey conducted among 564 Yemeni high school students reported that male students exhibited significantly higher WTC than their female counterparts (Al-Murtadha, 2021). This result was partially confirmed by Lee and Hsieh's (2019) study among university students in Taiwan. These disparate results suggest that the effects of gender and age on WTC may interact with other individual and situational factors, and their relationships may not be presumably constant.

4.2 Situational Factors Associated with L2 WTC

Given the prominence of promoting L2 learners' participation in educational settings, researchers and language educators have been unanimously focused on exploring situational factors that may boost or impinge learners' WTC. Hence, the majority of related studies were conducted in educational contexts. Kang (2005) pioneered a microlevel analysis of WTC among Korean students during conversations with native English-speaking tutors in a conversation partner program at a U.S. university. Utilizing video and audio recordings of the participants' conversations over eight weeks, semi-structured interviews, and stimulated recalls, Kang (2005) proposed that WTC is a dynamic situational concept emerging from the interaction of three situational variables (i.e., topic, interlocutors, and conversational context) and three psychological conditions of learners (i.e., excitement, responsibility, and security). This pivotal work by Kang (2005) has since informed many classroom-based studies on WTC.

Subsequent studies centering on classroom contexts have revealed a number of situational factors linked to learners' WTC (see Zhang et al., 2018). First, the interlocutor plays a significant role since typically learners were reportedly more willing to talk with familiar interlocutors who exhibited a supportive and proactive demeanor (Cao, 2014, 2014; Kang, 2005; Mystkowska-Wiertelak & Pawlak, 2017; Wei & Cao, 2021). In contrast, learners may experience a decrease in WTC when conversing with those who possess higher linguistic proficiency or greater knowledge on the topic under discussion (Mystkowska-Wiertelak & Pawlak, 2017; Yashima et al., 2018). That said, Nematizadeh and Cao's (2023) recent study indicated that challenging inter-locutors could sometimes generate a motivational force that triggered students' WTC. Additionally, Gallagher and Robins's (2015) social network analysis of forty-three international students at a British university found that students' WTC was remarkably enhanced when engaging in interactions among small groups composed of diverse ethnolinguistic backgrounds.   .

Topics and tasks, which are essential elements in the L2 class, can highly impact students' WTC (Cao, 2011; Cao & Philp, 2006; MacIntyre & Legatto, 2011; Mystkowska-Wiertelak & Pawlak, 2017; Peng, 2014; Wei & Cao, 2021). Intuitively, topics that are interesting, familiar, or personally relevant to students are likely to enhance WTC (Peng, 2012; Mystkowska-Wiertelak & Pawlak, 2017). Mystkowska-Wiertelak and Pawlak (2017) provided detailed descriptions of the associations between tasks and WTC in Polish EFL classrooms. They found that meticulously planned tasks with extended pre-task and post-task phases might inhibit students' WTC; conversely, tasks that provide greater latitude for creativity and spontaneous interaction tended to encourage greater WTC. Furthermore, they observed that productive activities, as opposed to receptive tasks like reading and listening, were more effective in promoting WTC (Mystkowska-Wiertelak & Pawlak, 2017). In addition, game-like activities or group projects were preferable (Cao, 2011; Eddy-U, 2015; Pawlak et al., 2016). These findings seem to boil down to the importance of learners' having things to say, a point emphasized by researchers (Ducker, 2022; Yashima, 2009). This suggests that learners are more inclined to express themselves in tasks that engage them with topics cognitively or experientially familiar to them.

In terms of how tasks are implemented, interactional patterns or classroom-organization modes are also linked to learners' WTC. Second language communication in classrooms typically occurs in dyads, groups, and whole-class situations. Previous research has indicated that students' WTC tended to be higher when interacting with peers, especially in dyads (Mystkowska-Wiertelak & Pawlak, 2017) or groups composed of three or four members (Cao, 2011; Cao & Philp, 2006; Wei & Cao, 2021), probably due to the lesser degrees of anxiety provoked in these situations. Yu (2015) specifically investigated how different interlocutor set-ups, based on learners' WTC levels, affected learners' language output. The learners' actual language output was measured by the number of words and the amount of turn-taking produced during the interaction. The results showed no significant difference in language output between dyads configured with learners with equivalent WTC levels (i.e., low–low, medium–medium, and high–high), and low–WTC learners' language output did not differ between different configurations (i.e., low–low, low–medium, and low–high). Finally, in teacher-led whole-class discussions, WTC may display more variability. While some students preferred this mode for its perceived enhanced learning potential (Zhong, 2013; see also Zhang et al., 2018), many others exhibited lower WTC due to various factors. Some of these factors are perceptions of lack of competence, fear of making mistakes, concern over losing face, desire to avoid conflicts with classmates, reluctance to dominate classroom communication, or avoiding being perceived as a show-off (Cao, 2011; Peng, 2012; Zhong, 2013).

Teachers and teaching practice are other salient factors that can modulate the magnitude of students' WTC in L2 classrooms. Teacher support, referring to "the teacher's help, friendship, trust, interest shown to students" (Peng & Woodrow, 2010, p. 843), is specified by Wen and Clément (2003) as a crucial element for Chinese EFL students' classroom WTC. Teacher support is an operational component of the concept of classroom environment that has been found to predict WTC (Khajavy et al., 2016; Peng & Woodrow, 2010). A specific type of teacher support, namely autonomy support grounded in Ryan and Deci's (1985) SDT, has been recently examined in WTC research. Zarrinabadi et al. (2021) defined teachers' autonomy support as the act of furnishing students with learning information while concurrently permitting students to utilize this information on their own terms. Their study unveiled both direct and indirect effects of teachers' autonomy support on WTC among 392 Iranian university students. Besides, other forms of teacher support such as emotional support (teachers' care and friendliness shown to students), instrumental support (teachers' practical aids such as time or services given to students), and appraisal support (teachers' evaluative feedback or advice given to students) have also been explored (Hejazi et al., 2023). These three aspects of teacher support were found to directly predict WTC (Hejazi et al., 2023).

Teacher immediacy is a salient concept in WTC research (Wen & Clément, 2003). This concept refers to teachers' verbal and nonverbal behaviors that foster proximity and close relationships between the teacher and students. Behaviors manifesting teacher immediacy, such as touch, relaxed postures, gaze, and gestures, were identified as predictors of WTC in a study of 235 students in Taiwan (Hsu et al., 2007). Fallah (2014) employed SEM in a study involving 252 Iranian university students. The results indicated that teacher immediacy indirectly predicted WTC through motivation and through shyness followed by confidence. Teachers' confirmatory or encouraging phrases, smiles, and eye contact were all embraced by the participants in Zarrinabadi's (2014) study as cues conveying teachers' sympathy and interest in students. These effects were paralleled by the impact of teaching styles characterized by humor and joke-telling (Peng, 2012). To some extent, these propositions and empirical findings are compatible with the results of WTC research framed from a multimodal perspective (Peng, 2019a; Peng et al., 2017), as discussed in Section 3.5.

In terms of teaching practice, the teacher's wait time, error correction, feedback, and even frequency of L2 use can to varying extents contribute to students' WTC. Wait time, defined as "the silent pause between a teacher's initiation and learner's response" (Zarrinabadi, 2014, p. 292), is typically esteemed by L2 learners. Extended wait time is generally favored by L2 learners, with anecdotal evidence suggesting its positive association with students' WTC (Peng, 2020a; Zarrinabadi, 2014). Teachers' corrective feedback is often categorized by the taxonomy of Lyster and Ranta (1997). This taxonomy classifies corrective feedback into several types: recasts, prompts (including clarification request, repetition, elicitation, and metalinguistic feedback), and explicit correction. These types can be viewed as positioned on a continuum ranging from implicit to explicit corrective feedback.

Divergent results have been reported on the influence of oral corrective feedback on WTC. For instance, explicit corrective feedback, specifically metalinguistic feedback and explicit correction, was evidenced to augment WTC (Tavakoli & Zarrinabadi, 2018; Zare et al., 2022). Yet, Zare et al. (2022) identified this effect as significant predominantly among high-proficiency Persian-speaking English learners. These two studies also yielded discrepant findings concerning the impact of recasts on WTC. Tavakoli and Zarrinabadi (2018) discerned no notable effect in their ten-week experimental study with ninety-six Iranian students, while Zare et al. (2022) detected a beneficial impact, particularly with high-proficiency participants who more readily grasped the corrective intention of teachers' recasts. Furthermore, Zare et al.'s (2022) interviews revealed that high-proficiency learners preferred explicit correction, while low-proficiency learners exhibited resistance, possibly perceiving it as an ego threat and thus a hindrance to their WTC. This finding echoes Zarrinabadi's (2014) observation that teachers' immediate feedback after errors could hamper WTC, whereas delayed error correction could enhance WTC. Cumulatively, these findings underscore the necessity of tailoring error correction to its timing and students' L2 proficiency levels.

A specific way of teaching and giving feedback, termed group-dynamic assessment (G-DA), was applied and its ramifications on WTC were scrutinized in Azizi and Farid Khafaga's (2023) recent experimental investigation. The G-DA refers to the practice where the teacher gives a student a prompt (e.g., repetition, explanations, or forced options), and redirects it to another student upon adjusting it as necessary to enhance comprehension. The instructional intent of G-DA is to transform individual learning challenges into collective learning opportunities, which can engage other students in the process. This study demonstrated that students who received instruction based on G-DA manifested notable gains in WTC compared to those in a control group.

Yang and Yin's (2022) study provides another detailed exploration of teaching practice with its unique focus on the concept of interpersonal projection (IP) in SFL (Halliday, 1978). The study investigated how teachers could enhance students' WTC by employing IP as a discourse strategy. Interpersonal projection is a meaning-making resource for inviting interlocutors to contribute their opinions, by means of linguistic devices (e.g., "Do you agree . . . ?", "Do you have any idea . . . ?"). Yang and Yin (2022) adopted an experimental design, incorporating IP into teacher questions in the experimental condition, while excluding IP in the control condition. The length and structural complexity of students' responses (i.e., speech output) were operationalized to reflect fluctuations of students' WTC in classroom interactions. The experimental results and interview data from this study confirmed that teachers' use of questions embedded with IP were correlated with high levels of students' WTC. Yang and Yin's (2022) study exemplifies an effective "marriage" of the theoretical insights and research approaches from both linguistics and applied linguistics, a point previously underscored in Section 3.5.

Classroom environment, atmosphere, or social climate is a broader situational factor, which is co-constructed by all parties in the classroom setting. Inspired by an ecological perspective, Peng and Woodrow (2010) incorporated classroom environment into a model that hypothesized several antecedents of WTC. Three essential components of the classroom environment were examined: teacher support, student cohesiveness, and task orientation. The three concepts refer to teachers' assistance, rapport, and vested interest shown to students, the degree to which students are acquainted with and help each other, and the importance placed on completing tasks and adhering to the subject matter plus the perceived relevance and utility of tasks. Peng and Woodrow (2010) found that the classroom environment predicted WTC directly and indirectly. These findings were confirmed in studies with students in Iran (Khajavy et al., 2016, 2018), Malaysia (Fatima et al., 2020), and Poland (Mystkowska-Wiertelak & Pawlak, 2017). Operationalizing classroom social climate by teacher academic support, teacher emotional support, and classroom mutual respect, Joe et al. (2017) found that classroom social climate indirectly predicted Korean secondary students' WTC via its effects on the satisfaction of basic psychological needs from the DST theory (Deci & Ryan, 1985). Additionally, de Saint Léger and Storch's (2009) qualitative study reported that a competitive and threatening classroom environment could intimidate students and inhibit their WTC. Therefore, creating a relaxed and supportive classroom environment is of paramount importance, particularly for EFL learners whose primary interaction with English occurs in the classroom. Furthermore, such an environment embodies a "positive institution," one of the three pillars of positive psychology as emphasized by Seligman and Csikszentmihalyi (2000). Positive institutions, along with positive subjective experience and positive individual traits, are the three pillars of positive psychology indispensable to individuals' well-being (Seligman & Csikszentmihalyi, 2000) and crucial in learners' L2 development (MacIntyre, 2016).

Before proceeding to the discussion of learning outcomes associated with WTC, it is pertinent to consider specific contexts that nurture various WTC profiles. One such context is study abroad (SA). Previous research has generally indicated that SA in the target language-speaking country can amplify learners' WTC, L2 proficiency, and frequency of L2 use (Kang, 2014; Yashima & Zenuk-Nishide, 2008). For instance, Yashima and Zenuk-Nishide (2008) demonstrated that students who participated in an SA program significantly surpassed their nonparticipating peers in WTC, L2 communication frequency, and scores on the Test of English as a Foreign Language. Similar gains in WTC were also observed among sixty Korean students who took part in eight-week SA programs in English-speaking countries. However, the qualitative investigation by Deng and Peng (2023), involving eight Chinese exchange students in Canada for one semester, revealed that SA did not invariably lead to WTC improvement. Instead, positive, negative, and no apparent changes in students' WTC were all detected, which was attributed to students' perceptions of values in speaking up, sense of fitting in, and classroom environment in the hosting university contexts. These findings conveyed important messages for educational administrators not to take for granted the assumed benefits of SA programs; rather, measures need to be taken to optimize the advantages of SA experiences for students.

Another distinct type of context is the multilingual context, especially where English is a viable communication medium besides the local language. This is elucidated in Henry and MacIntyre's (2024) book-length research, which aligns with recent "social" and "multilingual" turns in SLA and explores WTC in community settings. Henry and MacIntyre's (2024) work reports on a longitudinal qualitative study set in a migration context, where communication could occur in either Swedish (the target language) or English (the contact language). The research documented the changes in WTC in Swedish and English of eight women who migrated to Sweden and gradually developed proficiency in Swedish. Varied individual trajectories in WTC development were identified, subject to the influences of factors such as personal experiences, personality, circumstances of migration, and family situations. In addition, decisions about language choice were found to be influenced by various contextual and social factors. Based on the rich findings, Henry and MacIntyre (2024) proposed the 3D conceptualization model of WTC in multilingual settings, as presented in Section 2.2. Henry and MacIntyre's (2024) book contributes to a revised, updated understanding of WTC in community or multilingual settings.

4.3 Outcome Factors Associated with WTC

In comparison to the extensive body of research on the antecedents WTC, a considerately smaller number of studies have delved into the effects of WTC on linguistic or nonlinguistic outcomes. This represents a significant lacuna in this field, particularly given that the significance of WTC is predicated on its presumed ability to predict the frequency of L2 use, which in turn, may lead to improved L2 proficiency (Peng, 2022). The extant research seemed to present heterogeneous results in this regard. For instance, Joe et al. (2017) reported no correlation between WTC and L2 achievement, as evidenced in the final examination among Korean secondary school students. The authors posited that this absence of correlation could be because a higher WTC did not necessarily translate into tangible opportunities for L2 use. Similarly, Peng and Wang (2024) were unable to identify a significant predictive relationship between WTC and English public speaking performance among 134 Chinese college students enrolled in English public speaking classes.

Conversely, positive correlations between L2 WTC and L2 achievement have been reported (Al-Murtadha, 2021; Menezes & Juan-Garau, 2015). Menezes and Juan-Garau's (2015) investigation among Spanish secondary school students showed that higher WTC significantly predicted achievement levels. Al-Murtadha (2021) used observation data to operationalize observed WTC in class among twelve Yemeni high school students. Using Spearman rank-order correlation analysis, a substantial correlation was discerned between observed WTC and academic achievement manifested in classroom test scores. Zabihi et al.'s (2021) study among 100 Iranian university undergraduates also found that WTC significantly predicted these students' L2 English fluency rated by highly proficient L2 users, although WTC only accounted for 4 percent of the variance in perceived fluency ratings. With a specific focus on speech fluency, Wood's (2016) study revealed bidirectional relationships between L2 learners' WTC and fluency, which seems to suggest that there may be interplay between WTC and linguistic output. However, the limited scope of research in this line precludes a definitive conclusion regarding the role of WTC in learners' linguistic development.

With respect to nonlinguistic outcomes of WTC, a preliminary inference might suggest favorable impacts of WTC. Conforming to MacIntyre et al.'s (1998) L2 WTC model, WTC has been reported to predict the frequency of L2 use (MacIntyre & Charos, 1996; Yashima et al., 2004). In addition, Gallagher's (2013) study of 104 Chinese students attending a British university showed that WTC significantly mitigated the students' cross-cultural daily hassles reflected by communicating difficulties, social isolation, and time and financial constraints. In conclusion, given the limited and mixed results regarding the impact of WTC on linguistic and nonlinguistic outcomes in L2 learning, more substantial research is pressingly needed to fully understand and elucidate the role and implications of WTC in the L2 field.

5 Methodological Approaches in WTC Research

To unravel the trait-like, situated, and dynamic nature of WTC and its interplay with many other individual and contextual factors, quantitative methods (e.g., surveys and experiments), qualitative methods (e.g., interviews, observations), and the idiodynamic method have been employed, each of which can contribute to specific understandings of L2 learners' WTC, potentially functioning as pieces of a larger puzzle.

5.1 Quantitative Methods

Survey utilizing questionnaires is one of the most frequently used methods in WTC research. Following the quantitative paradigm in psychology research, WTC is often measured by scale items, which aligns with the conceptualization of WTC as a covert construct before overt communication (MacIntyre et al., 2001). Three major scales have often been used in the field. The first is the one adapted from the instrument measuring L1 WTC developed by McCroskey and Baer (1985). This scale contains twenty items measuring WTC with strangers, acquaintances, and friends across four communication contexts: public, meeting, small group, and dyad. This scale was reported to exhibit high reliability (Baker & MacIntyre, 2000; Ghonsooly et al., 2012). Compared to the items that describe many situations in daily encounters, another WTC scale by MacIntyre et al. (2001) specified situations inside and outside the L2 classroom. For each situation, the scale items measure L2 learners' WTC in four skill areas: speaking (eight items), writing (six items), reading (eight items), and comprehension (five items). Arguing that these items present communication situations not necessarily occurring in a foreign language context where the L2 is not used in daily encounters, Weaver (2005) used the Rasch model to develop a 34-item scale measuring WTC in speaking and writing in Japanese EFL classrooms. While this instrument is tailored to EFL classrooms, it should be noted that many items do not specify interlocutors (e.g., "Tell someone in English about the story of a TV show you saw"), which may result in various interpretations of the ambiguous wording. Despite this, with necessary adaptations, Weaver's (2005) scale has been utilized in several WTC studies in EFL contexts (Khajavy et al., 2016, 2018; Peng & Woodrow, 2010).

Survey data in WTC research have been primarily analyzed quantitatively, particularly for purposes of exploring the relationships of WTC with many other variables. Regression analysis (e.g., Amiryousefi, 2018; Dewaele, 2019; Lee & Lee, 2020a; Peng & Wang, 2024), path analysis (e.g., MacIntyre & Charos, 1996), and SEM (e.g., Joe et al., 2017; Khajavy et al., 2016; Peng, 2019a) are among the commonly used statistical methods. SEM is an extension of regression analysis and path analysis, allowing for the simultaneous testing of complex relationships between variables and the estimation of measurement errors (Hair et al., 2010).

Recent WTC research has displayed its interest in examining the mediating or moderating effects of learners' emotions or individual traits on the relationships between WTC and other variables (Lan et al., 2021; Lee et al., 2021; Li et al., 2022; Wang et al., 2021; Zhang et al., 2022). For instance, emotions such as L2 enjoyment, anxiety, and boredom (Li et al., 2022; Wang et al., 2021) or pride (Wang et al., 2021) were found to mediate the effects of classroom environment or class social climate on WTC. Enjoyment and anxiety also mediated the relationships between IDLE and L2 WTC (Lee et al., 2021, SEM). Boredom (Zhang et al., 2022) or along with enjoyment and pride (Wang et al., 2021) mediated the effects of language mindset on WTC. In addition, L2 grit was found to significantly mediate the relationship between the ideal L2 self and WTC (Lan et al., 2021). Apparently, these recent inquiries have arisen due to researchers' growing interest in positive psychology, particularly the role of positive emotions in SLA (MacIntyre, 2016). Investigating these mediating or moderating effects has deepened our understanding of the mechanisms behind L2 learners' psychological experiences, particularly how WTC interacts with a myriad of individual and contextual factors.

On the other hand, caution is warranted in interpreting the aforementioned relationships. Owing to the cross-sectional nature of many single-occasion surveys, the relationships modeled, whether obtained from regression analysis or SEM, are correlational and not necessarily indicative of causality. Mediation implies a process unfolding over time (MacKinnon, 2008). As O'Laughlin et al. (2018) pointed out, the detection of mediation processes necessitates temporally sequenced measurements of variables (i.e., predictors, mediators, and outcomes), and reliance on cross-sectional data for mediation analysis may result in biased estimates. Therefore, longitudinal designs and robust analytical methods, such as the cross-lagged panel model (CLPM) or its extended version, random-intercept CLPM (RI-CLPM; Hamaker et al., 2015) are needed for further exploration of mediational relationships in WTC research.

To probe dynamic changes in WTC while addressing the limitations of cross-sectional data, an innovative data collection method, known as experience sampling method (ESM) has been adopted in WTC research. The ESM is a tool used to collect real-time data on "what people do, feel, and think during their daily lives" (Larson & Csikszentmihalyi, 2014, p. 21). This was realized by asking participants to report on their current activities, thoughts, and feelings at regular intervals (e.g., every one hour), at the prompts of signals (e.g., a buzzer), or upon the completion of an event. These are referred to, respectively, as interval-contingent sampling, signal-contingent sampling, and event-contingent sampling (Hiver, 2022). This method is valuable in capturing the dynamic and context-dependent nature of human behavior and perceptions in a highly naturalistic and minimally nonintrusive manner. Khajavy et al. (2021) utilized ESM to explore the dynamic interplay between WTC, foreign language anxiety, and enjoyment among thirty-eight Iranian university students. They collected the participants' self-report data at ten time points every five minutes in six classes. The data were analyzed using moving correlation analysis of the three variables and a doubly multivariate ANOVA, which involves "more than one dependent variable measured on more than one occasion" (Khajavy et al., 2021, p. 177). The use of ESM enabled the researchers to identify significant variability in WTC, anxiety, and enjoyment both within weekly sessions and across different weeks. In brief, employing ESM to examine WTC represents a valuable avenue, as advocated by MacIntyre and Ayers-Glassey (2021). It is noteworthy that ESM is not necessarily a quantitative method, but allows for capturing individuals' subjective experiences by collecting participants' open-ended responses (Larson & Csikszentmihalyi, 2014).

In contexts where psychometric measures are used for gathering data over a period of time, a statistical method known as change point analysis (CPA) has been employed in WTC research (e.g., Henry et al., 2021a, 2021b). The CPA is a method for detecting abrupt intraindividual changes in "averages and/or standard deviations of variables" in a time series data (MacIntyre et al., 2017, p. 116) with a predetermined significance level (e.g., $p < .05$). This method uses bootstrapping for generating "confidence levels and confidence intervals for changes that are detected" (Henry et al., 2021a, p. 8). The resulting cumulative sum (CUSUM) charts offer visual representations of significant changes in a process. The CPA can be employed for tracking changes in multiple observations (i.e., variables) over time. For instance, in Henry et al.'s (2021a) study, CPA was used to explore significant changes in WTC in English (EWTC) and WTC in Swedish (SWTC), including their correlations among seven adult learners of Swedish within twelve months. Coupled with moving window correlation analyses that capture changes in the direction and strength of two variables in time series data (Verspoor et al., 2011), the use of CPA enabled Henry et al. (2021a) to identify various patterns in the development of WTC in the multilingual context. For instance, while a trend of increased SWTC and decreased EWTC was observed, significant shifts in WTC in the two languages occurred roughly at the same time among some learners while at different sequential orders for other learners. Change point analysis, which has been employed by other researchers in applied linguistics (Hiver, 2016; Nitta & Baba, 2015) and matches the CDST (MacIntyre et al., 2017), is instrumental in unveiling the dynamics of WTC in a longitudinal timespan.

Another quantitative approach to research WTC within the CDST framework is social networking analysis (SNA), which has been applied in a couple of WTC studies (Gallagher, 2019; Gallagher & Robins, 2015). The SNA is a methodological approach that examines the interdependencies among individual systems and their behaviors within an interconnected network structure. The analysis focuses on how nodes (individual actors within the network) and ties (relationships or interactions between these actors) are arranged and interconnected, which influence individual systems and the overall network (Hiver, 2022). Gallagher and Robins (2015) employed Exponential Random Graph Models (ERGMs) to explore the intricate relationships between different network formations (within the same cultural groups and between learners with diverse cross-cultural connections) and WTC of seventy-five students enrolled in an EAP program at a university in central England. The participants were prompted to name up to ten individuals with whom they had discussed significant matters in the past two weeks. The ERGMs resemble logistic regression in form, with the presence or absence of a network tie being predicted based on various structural effects and interactions between structure and individual attributes. Gallagher and Robins' (2015) study revealed that different situational subtypes of WTC were associated with various network tie patterns. Specifically, in large group settings, students with high L2 WTC were more popular within their own cultural groups, while cross-cultural ties were more likely to form between students with different levels of L2 WTC. In addition, individuals with high L2 WTC in small groups tended to be less active and popular among their intracultural peers. These findings indicated the complex role of social network structures in shaping WTC in cross-cultural settings.

Similarly, Gallagher's (2019) SNA study focused on the influence of network positions in terms of reciprocity (i.e., mutually acknowledged network ties) and brokerage (i.e., acting as intermediaries in social networks) on L2 learners'

WTC. An autologistic actor attribute model (ALAAM), which is a logistic regression method, was employed to analyze the data. The results showed that L2 WTC was positively predicted by "having more direct reciprocal ties that cut across cultural boundaries" (p. 206; i.e., a positive direct reciprocity effect) and by being involved in generalized reciprocal exchanges (i.e., a positive indirect reciprocity effect). However, reciprocal ties with non-classmates negatively affected L2 WTC. In terms of brokerage, negative effects were observed for individuals in brokerage positions. In addition, a positive flow betweenness effect was identified, suggesting that "being positioned between larger clusters in the network predicted greater WTC" (Gallagher, 2019, p. 206). These findings suggest complex interactions between social network patterns and L2 learners' WTC.

Another established approach is using experiments or quasi-experiments to test the effects of instructional intervention on L2 learners' WTC (Al-Murtadha, 2019; Luan et al., 2023; Munezane, 2015; Sato & Dussuel Lam, 2021; Yang & Yin, 2022). These instructional interventions include not only innovative teaching activities (e.g., visualization and goal-setting activities) but also microlevel teaching practice (e.g., the use of IP in pedagogic discourse and corrective feedback). These methods are rigorous in evaluating the effects of instructional intervention on students' WTC. For instance, Munezane (2015) conducted a quasi-experimental study with two experimental groups: one receiving visualization treatment (i.e., activities for visualizing oneself as English-speaking professionals) while the other participated in both visualization and goal-setting activities. A control group received regular content-based lessons. The results showed that the students receiving both types of treatment outperformed those in other conditions in terms of WTC. Other experimental studies have fine-tuned to the analysis of instructional language, such as the impact of IP in the teacher's discourse (Yang & Yin, 2022) and group-dynamic assessment as a unique way of feedback (Azizi & Farid Khafaga, 2023) on students' WTC, as presented in Section 4.2. Common statistical techniques for analyzing experimental data in these studies are Mann–Whitney U test (e.g., Yang & Yin, 2022), one-way analysis of variance (ANOVA; e.g., Munezane, 2015), and one-way analysis of covariance (ANCOVA; e.g., Luan et al., 2023).

While survey and (quasi)experiments have predominantly characterized WTC research within the quantitative paradigm, the following qualitative methods (i.e., interview, observation, learner journal, and focused essay) are also widely utilized, either in their own right or in combination with quantitative approaches. Therefore, mixed-methods approaches in WTC studies are not separately outlined in this Element to avoid redundance (since they are more or less combinations of quantitative and qualitative methods).

5.2 Qualitative Methods

Interview is a versatile tool for probing participants' subjectivity, and hence probably the most widely used qualitative method in WTC research. In particular, stimulated recall interviews have been frequently conducted to trigger students' recall of their WTC in lived communication scenarios (e.g., Cao & Philp, 2006; Deng & Peng, 2023; Kang, 2005; Mystkowska-Wiertelak & Pawlak, 2017; Reinders & Wattana, 2015; Shen et al., 2022; Wei & Cao, 2021; Yang & Yin, 2022; Zhou, 2023). A caveat in order is that stimulated recall interviews need to be conducted shortly after the communicative events observed or recorded, preferably within 48 hours after the events (Gass & Mackey, 2000), which is necessary for maximizing what can be recalled by the participants.

Observations are also often used, especially in classroom contexts. Nonparticipant observation (Dörnyei, 2007) is the common mode in WTC research for the purpose of minimizing intrusion to the L2 class. For instance, Cao and Philp (2006) developed a classroom observation scheme that consists of seven behavioral categories indicating high WTC or motivation (see also Cao, 2011). This observation scheme has informed a couple of subsequent studies (Peng, 2014; Zhou, 2023a).

At this juncture, the use of observation to obtain indicators of WTC warrants discussion in terms of the operationalization of WTC. Based on the literature, three ways of operationalization of WTC can be summarized: (1) scale items (e.g., MacIntyre et al., 2021, 2022), (2) observed communication behavior (e.g., Cao, 2011; Cao & Philp, 2006), and (3) observed discourse in terms of the number of turns (Yashima et al., 2018), number of words (Choe, 2017; Shen et al., 2022), and length and structural complexity (Yang & Yin, 2022) in learners' linguistic output. As recognized by Peng (2022), while the latter two ways would be helpful in alleviating difficulties in capturing students' WTC in situ, they deviated from the original conceptualization of WTC as a psychological process before overt behavior (MacIntyre et al., 2001). That said, researchers have argued that WTC can be reconceptualized as situated interactional activities (Ro & Burch, 2020) which hence can be manifested by learners' linguistic production. Research adopting the latter two options needs to explicitly articulate the research context and rationale for operationalizing WTC in a particular way, which can facilitate informed dialogue in the field (e.g., see Shen et al., 2022).

In addition, diaries, learning journals, or focused essays have often been obtained from L2 learners who are asked to record their retrospections. In MacIntyre et al.'s (2011) study, 100 junior high school pupils were requested to document in a focused essay a minimum of six scenarios of peak and low WTC. Zhou (2023b) collected five rounds of journals from six participants, which contain a learner self-assessment form for the students to reflect on the time in class when they most and least liked talking and their oral performance. The use of these qualitative methods enables researchers to get access to learners' perceptions and psychological processes on a regular basis without intruding into their lives (Dörnyei, 2007).

The analysis of qualitative data in WTC research has generally adhered to typical procedures in applied linguistics research, such as initial coding and second-level coding which entails iterative reading, coding, and interpreting the data (Dörnyei, 2007). In some studies, specific data analysis methods were described, such as qualitative content analysis (Cao, 2014; Cao & Wei, 2019; Deng & Peng, 2023; Peng, 2012; Zhou, 2023b), thematic analysis (Yang & Yin, 2022), a Grounded Theory approach (Ducker, 2022; Yue, 2014), or the analysis of teacher discourse (Yang & Yin, 2022), learners' speech output (Ducker, 2022; Yang & Yin, 2022; Yashima et al., 2018) or written output (Shen et al., 2022). Notably, the interpretive nature of qualitative data analysis necessitates strategies to bolster research reliability and validity. Within qualitative discourse, validity is often referred to as trustworthiness, authenticity, or credibility, defined as the accurateness of the findings from the viewpoint of the researcher, the participant, or the readers (Creswell & Creswell, 2022). Reliability and validity strategies employed in qualitative studies in WTC include cross-checking codes and/or calculating inter-coder agreement (Cao, 2014; Cao & Wei, 2019; Deng & Peng, 2023; Ducker, 2022; Peng, 2012; Zhou, 2023b), implementing member checking (Kang, 2005; Peng et al., 2017; Zhou, 2023b), providing triangulation and thick description (Zhou, 2023a, 2023b), or presenting negative evidence and contradictions (Zhong, 2013). These strategies are pivotal for ensuring the rigor and trustworthiness of qualitative inquiries.

5.3 The Idiodynamic Method

Grounded in the theoretical underpinnings of CDST, the idiodynamic method was advanced by MacIntyre and Legatto (2011). This method capitalizes on both quantitative and qualitative data and entails four major steps, namely recording, idiodynamic rating, stimulated recall, and transcription (for a practical guide, see MacIntyre & Ducker, 2022). Specifically, research participants first perform communication tasks, which are video-recorded. They are then invited to a stimulated recall interview, during which they watch the video recording of their task performance and rate their minute-by-minute WTC, using specially written software. The software allows them to adjust their WTC ratings between –5 and +5. Afterward, they get a printed graph of their WTC ratings and are prompted to discuss reasons for noticeable changes in their WTC with reference to specific video moments. These steps are all transcribed to facilitate the analysis of WTC fluctuations and their associated factors.

The idiodynamic method is considered compatible with the tenets of the CDST (MacIntyre & Ducker, 2022; MacIntyre & Legatto, 2011). In MacIntyre and Legatto's (2011) study, the participants were asked to complete a questionnaire that measures their trait-level WTC, anxiety, and personality in terms of extraversion. Hence, MacIntyre and Legatto (2011) identified four distinct timescales evident in their study. The first was long-term individual differences assessed by the questionnaire measuring trait WTC, extraversion, and language anxiety, which are developed over the years. The second is the scale of an hour, reflecting the interactions structured by the communication tasks in the laboratory. The third operated on a task-by-task basis that was measured in tens-of-seconds, while the fourth was on a per-second basis, capturing fluctuating WTC ratings that were a culmination of factors from other timescales. The parsing of timescales that accommodates WTC and its associated factors have enabled MacIntyre and Legatto (2011) to conclude that WTC can be seen as a dynamic system that shows intricate variation over time.

The idiodynamic method can be implemented using not only software but also a paper and pen technique. To maximize the accuracy of learners' recalls about their feelings in fleeting teaching moments, an instrument like a WTC grid for on-the-spot assessment of WTC can be an effective option (see Pawlak et al., 2016). However, its implementation requires careful consideration to minimize disruptions in the L2 classroom, particularly from intrusive prompts such as beeping sounds. To this end, the initial round of recording of classroom teaching could serve as a pilot phase, which allows the class group to acclimate to these prompts (see Peng, 2020b).

5.4 Three Illustrative Studies

It can be seen so far that WTC research has been continuously thriving and has utilized various perspectives and methods to elicit data. Next, three studies are presented as examples to illustrate that WTC research may be pushed forward. The rationale for presenting the three studies was driven by their novelty in disciplinary perspective, granular analysis of the links between WTC and learner talk, and cutting-edge vantage point. The first study (Peng et al., 2017) illustrated how SF-MDA-informed insights could be adopted to illuminate classroom WTC. The second one (Ducker, 2022) demonstrated a minute anatomy of how situated WTC translates or does not translate into learner talk. The third one (Tai, 2024) examined the effect of AI-supported interactions on L2 learners' WTC by means of experimental design.

5.4.1 Peng et al. (2017)

Peng et al. (2017) is a novel attempt to explore how multimodal affordances may mediate students' WTC in the L2 classroom. More importantly, this study focused on the multifaceted and semiotically-rich milieu of classroom dialogues, positing that students' WTC may be potentially an outcome of the interwoven meanings they co-construct via these multisemiotic resources. Using SF-MDA, they examined multimodal pedagogical discourse, encapsulating both the verbal and nonverbal semiotic mechanisms deployed for semantic construction within classroom settings. Specifically, this study addressed the two research questions:

(1) How are the experiential, interpersonal, and textual meanings embodied in the teacher's gestures in the two teaching scenarios invoking high and low WTC?
(2) How do the two scenarios differ in their discursive features constructed by language, gesture, and gaze intersemiotically and in the pedagogical effect respectively produced? (p. 309)

Participants

The participants of this study were four non-English major university students from an intact class in China and their English teacher named Ann (pseudonym). Ann is a native Chinese-speaking teacher who has been teaching English for more than twenty years. The curriculum goal for her class was to foster students' intercultural communication competence. Hence, oral interactions occurred frequently between Ann and her students and between the students.

Data Collection and Analysis

As argued by Peng et al. (2017), due to the ephemeral nature of multimodalities in pedagogic discourse (e.g., the teacher's smile, nodding, or gestures), it was difficult for students to comment on the influence of such multimodal cues on their WTC. Hence, this study adopted an alternative solution: teaching scenarios associated with the focal students' high WTC and low WTC were first identified. Following this, the experiential, interpersonal, and textual meanings embodied in the teacher's gestures in the two scenarios were analyzed against a related theoretic framework to answer the first research question. The discursive features constructed by language, gestures, and gaze were then analyzed to answer the second research question.

Three classroom sessions of Ann were observed and videotaped. These videos were then repeatedly analyzed to identify "critical incidents" (Kress et al., 2005) signifying potential changes in WTC, following specified guidelines from the literature. This yielded fifty-three, sixty-five, and forty-two clips from the three videotaped class sessions. Following each classroom observation, the four focal students were invited to participate in stimulated recall interviews, where they watched the video clips and rated their WTC during those scenarios on a 0–100 percent scale. The WTC scores from these students corresponding to the clips were then averaged to represent their WTC level in each of the clips, based on which scenarios with the highest (65 percent) and lowest (30 percent) WTC were pinpointed. It ended up that these two scenarios were from the same class session. The multimodal affordances present in these two scenarios were further analyzed by transcribing the interactions and annotating the multimodal affordances using the Multimodal Analysis Video software developed by the Multimodal Analysis Company (2013).

Analytic Framework

A framework for analyzing gestures was established based on Lim's (2011) and Hood's (2011) works. Experiential meaning realized in gestures was categorized as process, participants, and circumstances. Four types of "process" were discerned: state, material, behavioral, and mental. To elucidate, state processes denote static actions such as sitting; material processes exemplify tangible efforts like writing; behavioral processes encompass emotional (e.g., laughing) and physiological actions (e.g., coughing); and mental processes indicate cognitive activities, as seen when a teacher is reading the whiteboard. Gestures denoting objects were annotated as "participants" (i.e., persons or nonpersons). Gestures conveying spatial and temporal notions were annotated under "circumstances" as place and time, respectively.

Interpersonal meaning in gestures was classified into three aspects: attitude, engagement, and graduation, which is aligned with Martin and White's (2005) appraisal system. Attitudes were bifurcated into positive (e.g., a thumbs-up gesture) and negative (e.g., a forward-thrusting hand). Engagement hinges on the hand's orientation, where an open palm or palms facing upwards indicates a welcoming stance or opening for negotiation, contrasting with the authority undertone of palms facing downwards. Graduation was inferred from the gesture's velocity, categorized as fast or slow. Rapid motions communicate urgency and vigor, whereas slower gestures denote emphasis. Graduation was further coded by analyzing the duration of gestures observed during the playback of the video clip.

Textual meaning was construed through the rhythmic cadence of gestures, particularly beats and pointing. Beats serve to convey significance, with the frequency of the gesture's repetition coded as singular or multiple. Pointing, on the other hand, encapsulates aspects of directionality and specificity. The directionality of a pointing may be individual students, a display screen, or a nonspecific target like open space. The specificity of pointing is realized by the hand, fingers, or an instrument.

A framework for analyzing gaze was adapted from Tan's (2005) study. The teacher's gaze was classified into two categories: engaged and disengaged, differentiated by the presence or absence of a vector. A vector pertains to the directionality indicated by the teacher's gaze (Tan, 2005). In this study, the teacher's gaze was found to primarily focus on specific students, the entire class, or tangible items such as the whiteboard or textbook. In situations where the vector was indistinguishable or where the teacher's attention was introspective or cognitive, the gaze was labeled as disengaged.

Findings

As per the first research question, it was found that experiential meaning realized in gestures was predominantly conveyed through mental and material processes. Mental processes were more frequent in the high WTC scenario, accounting for 42.5%, compared to just 1.45% in the low WTC scenario. Conversely, material processes in the low WTC scenario (53%), which was marginally higher than that in the high WTC scenario (45%).

In terms of interpersonal meaning, positive attitudes were conveyed in the teacher's gestures in both scenarios with no indication of negative attitudes. The two scenarios differed in the embodiment of engagement and graduation. Gestural realization of contracting negotiation space was more prominent in the low WTC scenario (25%) than in the high WTC scenario (10%), suggesting that students' voices were more encouraged in the high WTC scenario. In terms of graduation, the high WTC scenario manifested more diversified frequencies of rapid gestures (12.5%) and low-positioned gestures (15.0%) than the low

WTC scenario (7.3% and 5.8%), which may function to "add dynamic to, and reduce the monotony of, the interaction" (Peng et al., 2017, p. 318).

Subtle differences in the gestural representation of textual meanings between the two scenarios were also spotted. More frequent gestures (17.5%) consisted of multiple rhythmic beats were found in the high WTC scenario than in its low WTC counterpart (5.8%), which may possibly reduce the monotony of peda-gogical interactions and capture students' attention more effectively.

Corresponding to the second research question, it was found that compared to the low WTC scenario, the high WTC one displayed more evenly distributed discursive exchanges and more adjacent moves between the teacher and the student. The teacher's verbiage, gesture, and gaze seemed to intersemiotically convey the teacher's care and sincerity to students, in a more consistent way than in the low WTC scenario.

Due to space constraints and the intricate theoretical foundation of this study, a comprehensive elaboration of details is beyond the scope of this Element. This study stands out for its pioneering approach of integrat-ing the exploration of multimodalities, grounded in linguistic theories, into WTC research. Such an integration sheds light on the subtleties of multi-modal interactions in L2 classrooms and their potential influence on variations in learners' WTC. As Peng (2019b) contended, while clear boundaries between linguistics and applied linguistics may be hard to pin down, the two domains usually adhere to distinct paradigms (e.g., empir-ically data-driven or theory-driven). Peng et al.'s (2017) study serves as a novel attempt to merge both disciplinary perspectives and hence to propel WTC research to transcend traditional reliance on learners' self-reports or researchers' external observations.

5.4.2 Ducker (2022)

Ducker (2022) recognized the growing interest in situational factors that impact the dynamic, situated classroom WTC. However, he pointed out a notable gap in the field, a limited understanding of how and when the arousal of WTC translates into actual classroom communication. Hence, Ducker (2022) explored the conditions under which the situated classroom WTC leads into observable classroom communication. Two research questions were raised:

RQ1. What is the relationship between situated moment-to-moment ratings of WTC and observable classroom communication?

RQ2. What factors impinge or enable the realization of learner talk from aroused situated WTC? (p. 221)

Participants

The participants of this study were recruited from a Japanese university EFL class in which domestic Japanese students were arranged to engage in interactions with non-Japanese students coming from other linguistic backgrounds. In this class, activities such as discussion, games, and group work were organized to provide students with ample opportunities to engage in free talk in English. However, the exact number of participants in this study was not specified.

Data Collection and Analysis

Six rounds of data collection were conducted. In each round, classroom interactions were video recorded to capture verbal and nonverbal communication related to WTC. Afterward, the participants underwent a ninety-minute interview during which they first rated their situated second-by-second WTC in classroom activities, using the idiodynamic software adjusted from MacIntyre and Legatto's (2011) version. In a follow-up stimulated recall session, they reported their feelings and thoughts tied to the self-ratings of WTC, and a semi-structured interview was conducted to gather background information on the participants' motivations and histories related to their WTC. In total, twenty-one classroom activities were recorded, and forty bilingual English–Japanese interviews were conducted.

Data collection and analysis in this study were "inductive, deductive, and recursive" (Ducker, 2022, p. 223). A focal point of the initial analysis was to explore the link between WTC and its actualization in classroom conversations. Two primary methods were used to examine the WTC–talk relationship: (1) correlation analysis using second-by-second data on WTC and realized communication, and (2) a qualitative review of WTC ratings and transcriptions of classroom activities against instances of talk, nonverbal actions, and nonlexical vocalizations. As the research progressed, the analysis oscillated between inductive and deductive processes, transitioning from developing initial codes to intermediate or axial coding. Upon iterative examining initial and intermediate codes, a grounded theory was built where a hierarchy was developed to delineate the interdependency of factors affecting WTC. Each factor's precedence was established, which was backchecked rigorously to ensure that each element in this hierarchy was consistent with the data. The author's colleague, an English teacher, was invited to involve in verifying selected data sets for accuracy.

Findings

Regarding the first research question, it was found that WTC and talk exhibited weak to moderate positive correlations or negative correlations in the results from different rounds of data. This suggested that instances where communication occurred were not necessarily preceded by aroused WTC or might even be associated with reduced WTC.

The second research question was explored through a grounded theory, which resulted in a hierarchical structure of factors influencing the WTC-talk relation. These factors span fourteen layers and are grouped into four main themes, from the bottom up: motivational forces, listening-related issues, topic-related issues, and language production issues. The base is formed by enduring motivations for studying English and situated motivations during classroom activities. Advancement through the hierarchy necessitates meeting the criteria of one layer before proceeding to the next.

Ducker's (2022) study has provided innovative insights into whether and how WTC is actualized in classroom interactions. Instead of going for brush-strokes by testing relations between participants' self-report WTC and communication frequency in a decontextualized manner, Ducker (2022) captured learners' actualized communication including talk, nonverbal actions, and nonlexical vocalizations in connection with situated WTC, both observed in real-time classroom settings. More importantly, while MacIntyre et al.'s (1998) L2 WTC model emphasized affiliation and control-oriented motives, Ducker (2022) identified a wider range of immediate communication goals in lived L2 classrooms, such as task completion obligations and turn-taking obligations. These perceived obligations could make learners to feel a "compulsion to talk" (Ducker, 2022, p. 235), a notion bearing resemblance to "forced participation" described by Wei and Cao (2021). Both notions denote learners' communication behavior prompted by perceived or tangible external pressures. This then raises the question: to what extent can such a psychological precursor to overt communication be considered "willingness" despite learners' potential "readiness" to enter discourse? This issue will be revisited in Section 7.

5.4.3 Tai (2024)

Tai's (2024) study represents recent fresh attempts to explore L2 learners' WTC in the AI-abound new era. Specifically, it examined the impact of out-of-class interactions with IPAs versus human interlocutors on EFL learners' WTC. Instead of simply tapping learners' subjective perceptions, this study conducted an intervention and adopted an experimental design to scrutinize the effect of interactions with IPAs on WTC. It addressed the following three research questions:

(1) Do out-of-class interactions with IPAs significantly increase EFL learners' WTC in English?
(2) How do the effects of out-of-class interactions with IPAs, L1 English speakers, and L2 English speakers on WTC differ?
(3) What factors influence WTC outside the classroom with IPAs, L1, and L2 English speakers? (p. 4)

Participants

The participants of this study included ninety-two first-year college students recruited from a university in Taiwan. They were split into three groups based on their interaction type: The IPA group of thirty-one students, who used a smartphone to interact with Alexa or Google Assistant; the EL1 group of twenty-nine students, who engaged with native English speakers, such as international students at their university; and the EL2 group of thirty-two students, who communicated with nonnative English speakers, such as their classmates, friends, and roommates.

Data Collection and Analysis

Tai's (2024) study adopted a mixed-methods approach. The three groups of participants were required to conduct two out-of-class interactions per week with their categorized interlocutors (i.e., IPAs, English L1 speakers, and English L2 speakers), each lasting about 10 minutes. This intervention lasted for twelve weeks. The IPA group submitted the screenshots of these interactions, and the EL1 and EL2 groups recorded the time they spent on the interactions and submitted the time logs at the end of the experiment. The participants' WTC was tested on three occasions, namely Test 1, Test 2, and Test 3 conducted before, during, and after the intervention. Focus group interviews were conducted at the end of the experiment to explore the participants' perceptions of the out-of-class activities and related effects on their WTC.

A two-way mixed-design ANOVA, that is, three rounds of WTC test and three groups (IPA, EL1, and EL2), and three separate one-way repeated-measures ANOVAs for each group were performed to provide answers to the first two research questions. In addition, an interpretive qualitative analysis of the interview data was conducted to answer the third research question.

Findings

In terms of the first two research questions, the results showed that while no significant differences in WTC between the three groups in Test 1, the IPA group scored significantly higher on WTC than the EL2 group in Test 2 and significantly higher than both the EL1 group and EL2 group in Test 3. The repeated-measures ANOVA on the three WTC tests for the IPA group also revealed significant results. These findings indicated that out-of-class interactions with IPAs significantly increased EFL learners' WTC in English. Based on the significant differences in WTC found between the three groups, it could be inferred that out-of-class interactions with IPAs had a greater effect on WTC than out-of-class interactions with L1 English speakers and L2 English speakers.

As for the third research questions, the qualitative analysis results showed that the differences in WTC between the three groups were influenced by a combination of contextual, individual, and sociopolitical factors. For the IPA group, "the mobility, convenience, interactivity, multifunctionality, and familiarity of IPAs on smartphones" (Tai, 2024, p. 1) were crucial. These elements enabled the learners to practice English flexibly, reduced their anxiety, and enhanced their engagement and confidence. Nevertheless, some participants in the IPA group also expressed concerns about automatic speech recognition resulting in errors and rapid pace of messages, and about irrelevant responses of IPAs. In contrast, interactions with human interlocutors (L1 and L2 speakers) were reportedly affected by factors such as the availability of partners, language proficiency levels, and the nature of the interaction, including the topics of conversation and the interlocutor's support and responses to errors.

Tai's (2024) study contributed empirical evidence showing that IPAs can serve as effective, low-stress tools for enhancing L2 learners' WTC. It has indicated promising avenues for expanding WTC research through the integration of digital communication tools into the fabric of future scholarly exploration, thus optimizing the benefits of technological advancements in facilitating L2 learning.

6 Implications for Enhancing L2 Learners' WTC

The theoretical tenets underlying the concept of WTC and numerous research findings have offered implications for promoting L2 learners' WTC. This should be a primary concern since theories need to be married to practice to ultimately benefit L2 learners. In this section, I will address implications drawn from the research reviewed previously, according to various contexts where L2 communication happens.

6.1 In In-Class Contexts

In the realm of language education, the classroom is the primary platform for L2 learners, especially for those learning the target language in a foreign language context. To enhance learners' WTC, L2 teachers can adopt various strategies. First, they can introduce authentic communication tasks that resonate with students' life experiences or aspirations. Each generation in specific social-cultural contexts may have its characterized interests and concerns, which can serve as the sources for teachers to update their lesson agenda when designing communication tasks in class. For example, seeking jobs in municipal cities or returning to hometown cities (Jin et al., 2022), or the advantages and disadvantages of choosing a disciplinary major (e.g., computer science or chemistry; Yang, 2018), have been pertinent topics for current students in the Chinese context. In addition, it is beneficial to nudge students into productive activities that elicit their linguistic output. Research has shown that these activities are more effective in prompting WTC than receptive tasks (Mystkowska-Wiertelak & Pawlak, 2017).

Second, classroom teaching dynamics need to be flexible, diverse, and rhythmic. Even with a prescribed lesson plan, it is suggested that teachers remain vigilant of students' responses and be prepared for spontaneous modifications. For instance, if prolonged pre-task and post-task stages inhibit students' willingness to talk, as noted by Mystkowska-Wiertelak and Pawlak (2017), these stages could be curtailed to rekindle students' interest and participation. Alternating configurations of pairs or groups enable students to meet diverse conversation partners, which can facilitate "fresh encounters" (Borzova, 2014). In addition, mandating students to move around and interview their peers on specific topics can activate the kinesthetic mode and invigorate the classroom atmosphere (Peng, 2019b). At the very least, teachers' use of gestures (e.g., multiple rhythmic beats) may function to introduce cadence to pedagogical discourse (Peng et al., 2017).

In terms of microlevel teaching practice, teachers might consider how to employ corrective feedback, wait time, and verbal and nonverbal cues to convey messages and build rapport with students. It is advisable for feedback, such as explicit correction, to be adopted with caution. It may be used with learners at higher proficiency levels (Zare et al., 2022) or within contexts where teacher support is clearly perceived (Peng et al., 2017); however, for learners at lower proficiency levels, explicit correction may be used judiciously. It is beneficial to avoid providing explicit correction immediately following learners' errors (Zarrinabadi, 2014). Other types of feedback, such as elicitation, can be used since evidence has shown that this type of feedback is most favored and considered most contributory to WTC (Zare et al., 2022). During whole-class interaction, it may be helpful for teachers to develop their tolerance of reticence from students, offering increased wait time upon raising prompts. Sufficient time for students to search for grammar or vocabulary, or even to rehearse their utterances can reduce their anxiety about speaking up and boost their WTC (Zarrinabadi, 2014). In addition, as previously emphasized, human communication is in nature multimodal. It could be useful for teachers to become adept at using multimodal cues, such as smiles, nodding, and palms-up gestures as well as inclusive language and IP (Yang & Yin, 2022) to construct teacher immediacy and support.

Teachers can also be mindful about building an active classroom atmosphere. At the beginning of a new semester, teachers can invite students to share their L2 learning and communication experiences, their concerns, or expectations, so that the class group can get acquainted with each other. The teacher might enhance group cohesion by setting *group norms* (Dörnyei & Murphey, 2003) oriented to promoting communication (e.g., applause for peers, no laughing at others' mistakes). In some cultures where the teacher is viewed as the authority in class and students' uninvited talk is uncommon, the teacher can infuse psychologically close feelings among students by adopting a relaxed or humorous teaching style, or even sharing their own struggles or failures in L2 communication situations (Peng, 2014). The empathy developed between the teacher and students can help alleviate students' concerns about hierarchy or perceived "power distance", thereby making them more willing to talk. Whatever efforts are exerted, promoting pleasant classroom experience or L2 enjoyment is advised as a priority in the L2 class, since such enjoyment has been widely found to lead to high WTC (Khajavy et al., 2018; Li et al., 2022).

6.2 In Out-of-Class Contexts

Promoting learners' WTC in out-of-class contexts needs to be emphasized by language educators. This is because the class time is limited and out-of-class contexts, when availed effectively, can function to sustain learners' WTC and thus enable L2 learning to take place beyond the classroom walls. One option for EFL teachers is to assign homework that requires oral practice or L2 communication outside class. Such homework may take the form of audio-visual speaking activities, where students record their oral answers to teachers' questions (Buckingham & Alpaslan, 2017) or team projects like interviewing international students in English about their cultural adaptation. The design of such assignments is aimed at simulating real-life language missions to foster students' WTC in authentic situations.

Another way is to offer various extracurricular or cocurricular activities to immerse students in an all-English environment. Activities (e.g., English Movie Nights) organized by student communities, such as English Corners and English Lounge (Peng, 2012), can be fruitful for promoting English communication on campus. As reflected by a participant in Peng's (2012) study, participation in a Halloween Party greatly enhanced this student's WTC. Such out-of-class activities can provide ample opportunities for students to savor authentic interaction opportunities, which are often more varied and spontaneous than classroom settings.

6.3 In Digital Contexts

Computer-mediated communication (CMC) has advanced fast in recent years, propelled by digital technology. Various online platforms (social media, language exchange apps, and online forums) have mushroomed. This creates unprecedented opportunities for promoting learners' WTC and L2 use in a virtual world not constrained by time and space. First, language teachers could encourage students to make good use of language learning apps (Peng & Wu, 2022; Zhang et al., 2024), computer games (Reinders & Wattana, 2015), or IPAs (Tai, 2024; Tai & Chen, 2023) that offer interactive and/or gamified experiences. Language learning apps often include features like speaking exercises, vocabulary games, and real-time feedback, which can make L2 communication more engaging and less intimidating. For instance, platforms like Tandem or Hello Talk have been found to contribute to language learners' motivation (Peng & Wu, 2022).

Second, utilizing DST as both a literacy-building tool (Shen et al., 2024) and a pedagogical tool may elevate learners' WTC (Luan et al., 2023; Shen et al., 2022). This could be implemented by allowing students to choose their own topics that resonate with their interests or experiences, craft their narratives, and leverage video editing platforms for narration (see Shen et al., 2022). DST activities may develop students' digital literacy while providing a contemporary and relevant way to practice speaking and listening skills. Teachers can also organize DST exchange activities with institutions in other countries, which can create a larger and more authentic platform for using English and transform the language learning process from merely an academic exercise into a gateway to global communication and intercultural understanding.

Similarly, online social media platforms (e.g., Facebook, WeChat, and WhatsApp) are useful sources for promoting L2 learners' WTC. These digital spaces offer students unique opportunities to put textbook language into real-world use. Involvement in virtual intercultural communications has been reported to have distinct effects on WTC (Lee & Lee, 2020a). More importantly, learners' participation in such online platforms enables them to experience the world connected by English or other languages, thus developing their international posture (Yashima, 2002). International posture or inclination toward an imagined community has been found to be crucial for generating L2 learners' WTC, surpassing constraints of the immediate environment (Peng, 2015; Yashima & Zenuk-Nishide, 2008).

7 Future Directions for WTC Research

WTC research has advanced theoretically and empirically over the past twenty-five years. From the review presented, future research may pursue several avenues. One is further exploration of the relationships between WTC and learners' L2 learning and behavioral outcomes, an area that still lacks substantial evidence. As addressed before, WTC is accorded significance since it is deemed to lead to increased L2 use, better learning performance, and positive nonlinguistic outcomes. To date, studies have shown mixed results regarding the impact of WTC on L2 learning achievement, which points to the need for more robust, particularly longitudinal, evidence. An emerging area of interest has focused on examining in microlevel classroom interactions whether and how WTC may translate into oral communication behavior (Ducker, 2022; Zhou, 2023a, 2023b) and its consequent benefits for L2 learning and communication. While the WTC-talk model proposed by Ducker (2022) portrays multilayers of factors intervening in the WTC-talk relationship (see also Zhou, 2023a, 2023b), the impacts of WTC and communication behavior on L2 development remain largely unexplored. In essence, the intricate links between WTC, talk, and language acquisition warrant further investigation.

Second, the growing interest in casual and/or mediational relationships between various variables and WTC underscores the necessity for longitudinal study designs (O'Laughlin et al., 2018). This is a viable research trajectory given that theories such as the broaden-and-build theory (Fredrickson, 2001) and the control-value theory of achievement emotions (Pekrun, 2006) have informed many studies that incorporated psychological constructs such as enjoyment, boredom, and grit into WTC research. However, cross-sectional data primarily reveal correlational relationships. Longitudinal or experimental designs are necessary to reveal processes that unfold over time, which is an important condition for establishing casual and/or mediational links. This also applies to studies on the impact of CMC or AI-powered communication on WTC, an area deserving increased research attention. Overall, advancing this field requires researchers to employ rigorous methodologies, innovative instruments, and advanced statistical analyses to yield precise results and deepen our understanding of WTC in relation to other individual and contextual variables.

Another distinct line of WTC inquiry is the exploration of its relationship with identity in multilingual contexts. It has been noted that many individuals today possess a plural linguistic repertoire (e.g., the local language, the global English, the heritage language; Wei, 2018). Therefore, in multilingual settings, the choice of language from this repertoire may be intimately connected to one's identity or language ideology (Henry & MacIntyre, 2024). Future studies may investigate how these associations are played out to influence L2 learners' WTC not just in multilingual societies but also in foreign language contexts and digital contexts.

Furthermore, future WTC research could greatly benefit from adopting interdisciplinary perspectives. Specifically, several studies have shown the effectiveness of combining systemic functional linguistics with empirical approaches commonly used in applied linguistics (e.g., Peng et al., 2017; Peng, 2019b; Yang & Yin, 2022). This integration can help reduce overreliance on learners' self-reports by supplementing them with a detailed analysis of the language that learners produce. This is compatible with the novel attempts made by researchers such as Ducker (2022) and Zhou (2023a, 2023b) who focused on exploring the WTC-talk connections. To advance in this direction, equipping researchers with linguistic theories and the skills for relevant analysis is not only necessary but also instrumental in expanding the scope of WTC research. Additionally, researchers may also take heed of a specific form of WTC, the "*silent yet yearning to speak up*" phenomenon identified in Peng's (2020b) study. This refers to a phenomenon in which learners are both ready and yearning to respond to the teacher's prompt, only to silently wait to be given the floor. Unlike using "hand-raising" as an indicator of WTC (Cao & Philp, 2006; MacIntyre et al., 1998), these students may not explicitly display overt action to signal their state of readiness. This may be particularly prevalent in Asian educational contexts, where students are refrained from speaking up unless they are nominated to do so. However, multimodal cues, such as eye contact or a smile directed at the teacher, could indicate a student's WTC. Probing this phenomenon could provide crucial insights important for L2 teachers to recognize and excavate this subtle form of WTC to the surface, thereby encouraging increased participation.

A final consideration pertains to the operationalization of WTC in non-English speaking contexts (e.g., China). Specifically, WTC was conceptualized as a state of "readiness" (MacIntyre et al., 1998). In English, the meaning of *readiness* may align closely with *willingness*, since *readiness* means "a state of preparation and prompt willingness" (Merriam-Webster, n.d.). In contrast, the Chinese equivalent of *willingness*, "*yiyuan*," implies an attitude or preference towards an activity, without necessarily suggesting readiness. This semantic discrepancy was observed when students affirmed their willingness to answer the teacher's questions but might not actually be prepared to do so when given the opportunity (Peng, 2020b). It is likely that such semantic discrepancy may exist in other languages, an issue warranting further attention. Therefore, it is crucial for researchers to clarify to learners the specific conceptualization of WTC at the onset when collecting self-report data from EFL learners. This clarity is necessary to ensure alignment between the researcher's and participants' understanding of this key concept and thereby avoid potential misinterpretations.

References

Al-Murtadha, M. A. (2019). Enhancing EFL learners' willingness to communicate with visualization and goal-setting activities. *TESOL Quarterly, 53*(1), 133–157. https://doi.org/10.1002/tesq.474.

Al-Murtadha, M. A. (2021). The relationships among self-reported and observed first language and second language willingness to communicate and academic achievement. *Language, Culture and Curriculum, 34*(1), 80–94. https://doi.org/10.1080/07908318.2020.1727495.

Amiryousefi, M. (2018). Willingness to communicate, interest, motives to communicate with the instructor, and L2 speaking: A focus on the role of age and gender. *Innovation in Language Learning and Teaching, 12*(3), 221–234. https://doi.org/10.1080/17501229.2016.1170838.

Azizi, Z., & Farid Khafaga, A. (2023). Scaffolding via group-dynamic assessment to positively affect motivation, learning anxiety, and willingness to communicate: A case study of high school students. *Journal of Psycholinguistic Research, 52*(3), 831–851. https://doi.org/10.1007/s10936-023-09935-6.

Baker, S. C., & MacIntyre, P. D. (2000). The role of gender and immersion in communication and second language orientations. *Language Learning, 50*(2), 311–341. https://doi.org/10.1111/0023-8333.00119.

Bennett, S. (2012). Digital natives. In Z. Yan (Ed.), *Encyclopedia of cyber behavior* (pp. 212–219). IGI Global.

Bisson, M.-J., Heuven, W. J. B., Conklin, K., & Tunney, R. J. (2014). The role of repeated exposure to multimodal input in incidental acquisition of foreign language vocabulary. *Language Learning, 64*(4), 855–877. https://doi.org/10.1111/lang.12085.

Borzova, E. (2014). Mingles in the foreign language classroom. *English Teaching Forum, 52*(2), 20–27.

Bronfenbrenner, U. (1979). *The ecology of human development.* Harvard University Press.

Bronfenbrenner, U. (1993). The ecology of cognitive development: Research models and fugitive findings. In R. H. Wozniak & K. W. Fischer (Eds.), *Development in context: Acting and thinking in specific environments* (pp. 3–44). Lawrence Erlbaum Associates.

Buckingham, L., & Alpaslan, R. S. (2017). Promoting speaking proficiency and willingness to communicate in Turkish young learners of English through asynchronous computer-mediated practice. *System*, *65*, 25–37. https://doi.org/10.1016/j.system.2016.12.016.

Burgoon, J. K. (1976). The unwillingness-to-communicate: Development and validation. *Communication Monographs*, *43*(1), 60–69. https://doi.org/10.1080/03637757609375916.

Cao, Y. (2011). Investigating situational willingness to communicate within second language classrooms from an ecological perspective. *System*, *39*(4), 468–479. https://doi.org/10.1016/j.system.2011.10.016.

Cao, Y. (2014). A sociocognitive perspective on second language classroom willingness to communicate. *TESOL Quarterly*, *48*(4), 789–814. https://doi.org/10.1002/tesq.155.

Cao, Y., & Philp, J. (2006). Interactional context and willingness to communicate: A comparison of behavior in whole class, group and dyadic interaction. *System*, *34*(4), 480–493. https://doi.org/10.1016/j.system.2006.05.002.

Cao, Y., & Wei, W. (2019). Willingness to communicate from an English as an International Language (EIL) perspective: The case of Macau. *System*, *87*, 102149. https://doi.org/10.1016/j.system.2019.102149.

Choe, A. T. (2017). Exploring the dynamics of willingness to communicate in written communication: A case study. *Working Papers in TESOL & Applied Linguistics*, *17*(1), 39–55.

Cortazzi, M., & Jin, L. (1996). Cultures of learning: Language classrooms in China. In H. Coleman (Ed.), *Society and the language classroom* (pp. 169–206). Cambridge University Press.

Creswell, J. W., & Creswell, J. D. (2022). *Research design: Qualitative, quantitative, and mixed methods approaches* (6th ed.). Sage.

de Saint Léger, D., & Storch, N. (2009). Learners' perceptions and attitudes: Implications for willingness to communicate in an L2 classroom. *System*, *37*(2), 269–285. https://doi.org/10.1016/j.system.2009.01.001.

Deci, E. L., & Ryan, R. M. (1985). *Intrinsic motivation and self-determination in human behavior*. Plenum.

Deng, F., & Peng, J. (2023). Sustaining short-term exchange students' willingness to communicate in second language in multilingual classrooms. *RELC Journal*, *54*(3), 683–696. https://doi.org/10.1177/00336882211035590.

Denies, K., Yashima, T., & Janssen, R. (2015). Classroom versus societal willingness to communicate: Investigating French as a second language in Flanders. *The Modern Language Journal*, *99*(4), 718–739. https://doi.org/10.1111/modl.12276.

Dewaele, J.-M. (2019). The effect of classroom emotions, attitudes toward English, and teacher behavior on willingness to communicate among

English foreign language learners. *Journal of Language and Social Psychology, 38*(4), 523–535. https://doi.org/10.1177/0261927x19864996.

Dewaele, J.-M., & MacIntyre, P. (2014). The two faces of Janus? Anxiety and enjoyment in the foreign language classroom. *Studies in Second Language Learning and Teaching, 4*, 237–274. https://doi.org/10.14746/ssllt.2014.4.2.5.

Donovan, L. A., & MacIntyre, P. D. (2004). Age and sex differences in willingness to communicate, communication apprehension, and self-perceived competence. *Communication Research Reports, 21*(4), 420–427. https://doi.org/10.1080/08824090.

Dörnyei, Z. (2005). *The psychology of the language learner: Individual differences in second language acquisition.* Lawrence Erlbaum Associates.

Dörnyei, Z. (2007). *Research methods in applied linguistics: Quantitative, qualitative, and mixed methodologies.* Oxford University Press.

Dörnyei, Z., & Murphey, T. (2003). *Group dynamics in the language classroom.* Cambridge University Press.

Ducker, N. T. (2022). Bridging the gap between willingness to communicate and learner talk. *The Modern Language Journal, 106*(1), 216–244. https://doi.org/10.1111/modl.12764.

Dweck, C. S. (1999). *Self-theories: Their role in motivation, personality, and development.* Psychology Press.

Eddy-U, M. (2015). Motivation for participation or non-participation in group tasks: A dynamic systems model of task-situated willingness to communicate. *System, 50*, 43–55. https://doi.org/10.1016/j.system.2015.03.005.

Fallah, N. (2014). Willingness to communicate in English, communication self-confidence, motivation, shyness and teacher immediacy among Iranian English-major undergraduates: A structural equation modeling approach. *Learning and Individual Differences, 30*, 140–147. https://doi.org/10.1016/j.lindif.2013.12.006.

Fatima, I., Ismail, S. A. M. M., Pathan, Z. H., & Memon, U. (2020). The power of openness to experience, extraversion, L2 self-confidence, classroom environment in predicting L2 willingness to communicate. *International Journal of Instruction, 13*(3), 909–924. https://doi.org/10.29333/iji.2020.13360a.

Fattahi, N., Ebn-Abbasi, F., Botes, E., & Nushi, M. (2023). Nothing ventured, nothing gained: The impact of enjoyment and boredom on willingness to communicate in online foreign language classrooms. *Language Teaching Research*, Advance online publication. https://doi.org/10.1177/13621688231194286.

Feng, E., Wang, Y., & King, R. B. (2023). Achievement goals, emotions and willingness to communicate in EFL learning: Combining variable- and person-centered approaches. *Language Teaching Research*, Advance online publication. https://doi.org/10.1177/13621688221146887.

Fredrickson, B. L. (2001). The role of positive emotions in positive psychology: The broaden-and-build theory of positive emotions. *American Psychologist*, *56*(3), 218–226. https://doi.org/10.1037//0003-066x.56.3.218.

Fushino, K. (2010). Causal relationships between communication confidence, beliefs about group work, and willingness to communicate in foreign language group work. *TESOL Quarterly*, *44*(4), 700–724. https://doi.org/10.5054/tq.2010.235993.

Gallagher, H. C. (2013). Willingness to communicate and cross-cultural adaptation: L2 communication and acculturative stress as transaction. *Applied Linguistics*, *34*(1), 53–73. https://doi.org/10.1093/applin/ams023.

Gallagher, H. C. (2019). Social networks and the willingness to communicate: Reciprocity and brokerage. *Journal of Language and Social Psychology*, *38* (2), 194–214. https://doi.org/10.1177/0261927X18809146.

Gallagher, H. C., & Robins, G. (2015). Network statistical models for language learning contexts: Exponential random graph models and willingness to communicate. *Language Learning*, *65*(4), 929–962. https://doi.org/10.1111/lang.12130.

Gardner, R. C. (1985). *Social psychology and second language learning: The role of attitude and motivation*. Edward Arnold.

Gardner, R. C., & MacIntyre, P. D. (1993). On the measurement of affective variables in second language learning. *Language Learning*, *43*(2), 157–194. https://doi.org/10.1111/j.1467-1770.1992.tb00714.x.

Gass, S. M., & Mackey, A. (2000). *Stimulated recall methodology in second language research*. Lawrence Erlbaum Associates.

Ghonsooly, B., Khajavy, G. H., & Asadpour, S. F. (2012). Willingness to communicate in English among Iranian non-English major university students. *Journal of Language and Social Psychology*, *31*(2), 197–211. https://doi.org/10.1177/0261927X12438538.

Goldberg, L. R. (2012). The development of markers for the Big-Five factor structure. *Psychological Assessment*, *4*(1), 26–42. https://doi.org/10.1037/1040-3590.4.1.26.

Hair, J. F., Black, W. C., Babin, B. J., & Anderson, R. E. (2010). *Multivariate data analysis* (7th ed.). Prentice Hall.

Halliday, M. A. K. (1978). *Language as social semiotic: The social interpretation of language and meaning*. Edward Arnold.

Hamaker, E. L., Kuiper, R. M., & Grasman, R. P. P. P. (2015). A critique of the cross-lagged panel model. *Psychological Methods*, *20*(1), 102–116. https://doi.org/10.1037/a0038889.

Hejazi, S. Y., Sadoughi, M., & Peng, J. (2023). The structural relationship between teacher support and willingness to communicate: The mediation of L2 anxiety and the moderation of growth language mindset. *Journal of Psycholinguistic Research, 52*, 2955–2978. https://doi.org/10.1007/s10936-023-10026-9.

Henry, A., & MacIntyre, P. D. (2024). *Willingness to communicate, multilingualism and interactions in community contexts.* Multilingual Matters.

Henry, A., Thorsen, C., & MacIntyre, P. D. (2021a). Willingness to communicate in a multilingual context: Part one, a time-serial study of developmental dynamics. *Journal of Multilingual and Multicultural Development*, Advance online publication. https://doi.org/10.1080/01434632.2021.1931248.

Henry, A., Thorsen, C., & MacIntyre, P. D. (2021b). Willingness to communicate in a multilingual context: Part two, person-context dynamics. *Journal of Multilingual and Multicultural Development*, Advance online publication. https://doi.org/10.1080/01434632.2021.1935975.

Hiver, P. (2015). Attractor states. In Z. Dörnyei, P. D. MacIntyre, & A. Henry (Eds.), *Motivational dynamics in language learning* (pp. 20–28). Multilingual Matters.

Hiver, P. (2016). The triumph over experience: Hope and hardiness in novice L2 teachers. In P. D. MacIntyre, T. Gregersen, & S. Mercer (Eds.), *Positive psychology in SLA* (pp. 168–192). Multilingual Matters.

Hiver, P. (2022). Methods for complexity theory in individual differences research. In S. Li, P. Hiver, & M. Papi (Eds.), *The Routledge handbook of second language acquisition and individual differences* (pp. 477–493). Routledge.

Holsanova, J. (2012). New methods for studying visual communication and multimodal integration. *Visual Communication, 11*(3), 251–257. https://doi.org/10.1177/1470412912446558.

Hood, S. (2011). Body language in face-to-face teaching: A focus on textual and interpersonal meaning. In S. Dreyfus, S. Hood, & M. Stenglin (Eds.), *Semiotic margins: Meaning in multimodalities* (pp. 31–52). Continuum.

Hsieh, W.-M., Yeh, H.-C., & Chen, N.-S. (2023). Impact of a robot and tangible object (R&T) integrated learning system on elementary EFL learners' English pronunciation and willingness to communicate. *Computer Assisted Language Learning*, Advance online publication. https://doi.org/10.1080/09588221.2023.2228357.

Hsu, L.-I., Watson, T., Lin, C.-H., & Ho, T.-C. (2007). Explorations in teachers' nonverbal immediacy behaviors and students' willingness to talk in English. *English Teaching and Learning, 31*(1), 1–27. https://doi.org/10.6330/ETL.2007.31.3.01.

Hu, G. (2002). Potential cultural resistance to pedagogical imports: The case of communicative language teaching in China. *Language, Culture and Curriculum, 15*(2), 93–105. https://doi.org/10.1080/07908310208666636.

Huang, H.-T. D. (2023). Examining the effect of digital storytelling on English speaking proficiency, willingness to communicate, and group cohesion. *TESOL Quarterly, 57*(1), 242–269. https://doi.org/10.1002/tesq.3147.

Jeon, J., Lee, S., & Choe, H. (2023). Beyond ChatGPT: A conceptual framework and systematic review of speech-recognition chatbots for language learning. *Computers & Education, 206*, Article 104898. https://doi.org/10.1016/j.compedu.2023.104898.

Jin, C., Li, B., Jansen, S. J., Boumeester, H. J., & Boelhouwer, P. J. (2022). What attracts young talents? Understanding the migration intention of university students to first-tier cities in China. *Cities, 128*, 103802. https://doi.org/10.1016/j.cities.2022.103802.

Joe, H.-K., Hiver, P. H., & Al-Hoorie, A. H. (2017). Classroom social climate, self-determined motivation, willingness to communicate, and achievement: A study of structural relationships in instructed second language settings. *Learning and Individual Differences, 53*, 133–144. https://doi.org/10.1016/j.lindif.2016.11.005.

Kang, D.-M. (2014). The effects of study-abroad experiences on EFL learners' willingness to communicate, speaking abilities, and participation in classroom interaction. *System, 42*, 319–332. https://doi.org/10.1016/j.system.2013.12.025.

Kang, S.-J. (2005). Dynamic emergence of situational willingness to communicate in a second language. *System, 33*(2), 277–292. https://doi.org/10.1016/j.system.2004.10.004.

Kessler, M. (2022). Multimodality. *ELT Journal, 76*(4), 551–554. https://doi.org/10.1093/elt/ccac028.

Khajavy, G. H., Ghonsooly, B., Fatemi, A. H., & Choi, C. W. (2016). Willingness to communicate in English: A microsystem model in the Iranian EFL classroom context. *TESOL Quarterly, 50*(1), 154–180. https://doi.org/10.1002/tesq.204.

Khajavy, G. H., MacIntyre, P. D., & Barabadi, E. (2018). Role of the emotions and classroom environment in willingness to communicate: Applying doubly latent multilevel analysis in second language acquisition research. *Studies in Second Language Acquisition, 40*(3), 605–624. https://doi.org/10.1017/S0272263117000304.

Khajavy, G. H., MacIntyre, P. D., & Taherian, T. (2021). Examining the dynamic relationships between willingness to communicate, anxiety and enjoyment using the experience sampling method. In N. Zarrinabadi &

M. Pawlak (Eds.), *New perspectives on willingness to communicate in a second language* (pp. 169–197). Springer.

Kress, G. (2010). *Multimodality: A social semiotic approach to contemporary communication*. Routledge.

Kress, G., Jewitt, C., Bourne, J. et al. (2005). *English in urban classrooms: A multimodal perspective on teaching and learning*. Routledge.

Kress, G., & van Leeuwen, T. (2006). *Reading images: The grammar of visual design* (2nd ed.). Routledge.

Lan, G., Nikitina, L., & Woo, W. S. (2021). Ideal L2 self and willingness to communicate: A moderated mediation model of shyness and grit. *System, 99*, 102503. https://doi.org/10.1016/j.system.2021.102503.

Larsen-Freeman, D., & Cameron, L. (2008). *Complex systems and applied linguistics*. Oxford University Press.

Larson, R., & Csikszentmihalyi, M. (2014). The experience sampling method. In M. Csikszentmihalyi (Ed.), *Flow and the foundations of positive psychology: The collected works of Mihaly Csikszentmihalyi* (pp. 21–34). Springer.

Lee, J. S., & Drajati, N. A. (2020). Willingness to communicate in digital and non-digital EFL contexts: Scale development and psychometric testing. *Computer Assisted Language Learning, 33*(7), 688–707. https://doi.org/10.1080/09588221.2019.1588330.

Lee, J. S., & Hsieh, J. C. (2019). Affective variables and willingness to communicate of EFL learners in in-class, out-of-class, and digital contexts. *System, 82*, 63–73. https://doi.org/10.1016/j.system.2019.03.002.

Lee, J. S., & Lee, K. (2020a). Affective factors, virtual intercultural experiences, and L2 willingness to communicate in in-class, out-of-class, and digital settings. *Language Teaching Research, 24*(6), 813–833. https://doi.org/10.1177/1362168819831408.

Lee, J. S., & Lee, K. (2020b). Role of L2 motivational self system on willingness to communicate of Korean EFL university and secondary students. *Journal of Psycholinguistic Research, 49*(1), 147–161. https://doi.org/10.1007/s10936-019-09675-6.

Lee, J. S., & Lu, Y. (2023). L2 motivational self system and willingness to communicate in the classroom and extramural digital contexts. *Computer Assisted Language Learning, 36*(1–2), 126–148. https://doi.org/10.1080/09588221.2021.1901746.

Lee, J. S., Sylvén, L. K., & Lee, K. (2021). Cross-cultural insights into Korean and Swedish secondary school students' willingness to communicate in a second language. *Journal of Multilingual and Multicultural Development, 42*(6), 522–536. https://doi.org/10.1080/01434632.2019.1708917.

Lee, J. S., Xie, Q., & Lee, K. (2021). Informal digital learning of English and L2 willingness to communicate: Roles of emotions, gender, and educational stage. *Journal of Multilingual and Multicultural Development*, Advance online publication. https://doi.org/10.1080/01434632.2021.1918699.

Li, C., Dewaele, J.-M., Pawlak, M., & Kruk, M. (2022). Classroom environment and willingness to communicate in English: The mediating role of emotions experienced by university students in China. *Language Teaching Research*, Advance online publication. https://doi.org/10.1177/13621688221111623.

Liang, J.-C., Hwang, G.-J., Chen, M.-R. A., & Darmawansah, D. (2021). Roles and research foci of artificial intelligence in language education: An integrated bibliographic analysis and systematic review approach. *Interactive Learning Environments*, Advance online publication. https://doi.org/10.1080/10494820.2021.1958348.

Lim, F. V. (2011). *A systemic functional multimodal discourse analysis approach to pedagogic discourse*. (Unpublished doctoral thesis). National University of Singapore, Singapore.

Lim, F. V. (2021). *Designing learning with embodied teaching*. Routledge.

Lin, V., Yeh, H.-C., Huang, H.-H., & Chen, N.-S. (2022). Enhancing EFL vocabulary learning with multimodal cues supported by an educational robot and an IoT-Based 3D book. *System*, *104*, Article 102691. https://doi.org/10.1016/j.system.2021.102691.

Lin, Y.-T. (2019). Taiwanese EFL learners' willingness to communicate in English in the classroom: Impacts of personality, affect, motivation, and communication confidence. *The Asia-Pacific Education Researcher*, *28*(2), 101–113. https://doi.org/10.1007/s40299-018-0417-y.

Littlewood, W. (1981). *Communicative language teaching: An introduction*. Cambridge University Press.

Liu, J. (2002). Negotiating silence in American classrooms: Three Chinese cases. *Language and Intercultural Communication*, *2*(1), 37–54. https://doi.org/10.1080/14708470208668074.

Liu, M., & Jackson, J. (2008). An exploration of Chinese EFL learners' unwillingness to communicate and foreign language anxiety. *The Modern Language Journal*, *92*(1), 71–86. https://doi.org/10.1111/j.1540-4781.2008.00687.x.

Liu, G., & Ma, C. (2023). Measuring EFL learners' use of ChatGPT in informal digital learning of English based on the technology acceptance model. *Innovation in Language Learning and Teaching*, *18*(2), 125–138. https://doi.org/10.1080/17501229.2023.2240316.

Lou, N. M., & Noels, K. A. (2019). Promoting growth in foreign and second language education: A research agenda for mindsets in language learning and teaching. *System*, *86*, Article 102126. https://doi.org/10.1016/j.system .2019.102126.

Luan, L., Yi, Y., Hwang, G.-J. et al. (2023). Facilitating EFL learners' willingness to communicate amidst the pandemic: A digital storytelling-based online flipped learning approach. *Innovation in Language Learning and Teaching*, Advance online publication. https://doi.org/10.1080/17501229 .2023.2241436.

Lyster, R., & Ranta, L. (1997). Corrective feedback and learner uptake: Negotiation of form in communicative classrooms. *Studies in Second Language Acquisition*, *19*(1), 37–66. https://doi.org/10.1017/S0272263197001034.

MacIntyre, P. D. (2016). So far so good: An overview of positive psychology and its contributions to SLA. In D. Gabryś-Barker & D. Gałajda (Eds.), *Positive psychology perspectives on foreign language learning and teaching* (pp. 3–20). Springer.

MacIntyre, P. D. (2020). Expanding the theoretical base for the dynamics of willingness to communicate. *Studies in Second Language Learning and Teaching*, *10*(1), 111–131. https://doi.org/10.14746/ssllt.2020.10.1.6.

MacIntyre, P. D., & Ayers-Glassey, S. (2021). Measuring willingness to communicate. In P. Winke & T. Brunfaut (Eds.), *The Routledge handbook of second language acquisition and language testing* (pp. 187–197). Routledge.

MacIntyre, P. D., Baker, S. C., Clément, R., & Conrod, S. (2001). Willingness to communicate, social support, and language-learning orientations of immersion students. *Studies in Second Language Acquisition*, *23*(3), 369–388. https://doi.org/10.1017/S0272263101003035.

MacIntyre, P. D., Baker, S. C., Clément, R., & Donovan, L. A. (2002). Sex and age effects on willingness to communicate, anxiety, perceived competence, and L2 motivation among junior high school French immersion students. *Language Learning*, *52*(3), 537–564. https://doi.org/10.1111/1467-9922.00226.

MacIntyre, P. D., Baker, S. C., Clément, R., & Donovan, L. A. (2003). Talking in order to learn: Willingness to communicate and intensive language programs. *Canadian Modern Language Review*, *59*(4), 589–607. https:// doi.org/10.3138/cmlr.59.4.589.

MacIntyre, P. D., & Blackie, R. A. (2012). Action control, motivated strategies, and integrative motivation as predictors of language learning affect and the intention to continue learning French. *System*, *40*, 533–543. https://doi.org/ 10.1016/j.system.2012.10.014.

MacIntyre, P. D., & Charos, C. (1996). Personality, attitudes, and affect as predictors of second language communication. *Journal of Language and Social Psychology, 15*(1), 3–26. https://doi.org/10.1177/0261927X960151001.

MacIntyre, P. D., Dörnyei, Z., Clément, R., & Noels, K. A. (1998). Conceptualizing willingness to communicate in a L2: A situational model of L2 confidence and affiliation. *The Modern Language Journal, 82*(4), 545–562. https://doi.org/10.1111/j.1540-4781.1998.tb05543.x.

MacIntyre, P. D., & Ducker, N. (2022). The idiodynamic method: A practical guide for researchers. *Research Methods in Applied Linguistics, 1*(2), Article 100007. https://doi.org/10.1016/j.rmal.2022.100007.

MacIntyre, P. D., Gregersen, T., & Mercer, S. (Eds.). (2016). *Positive psychology in SLA*. Multilingual Matters.

MacIntyre, P. D., & Legatto, J. J. (2011). A dynamic system approach to willingness to communicate: Developing an idiodynamic method to capture rapidly changing affect. *Applied Linguistics, 32*(2), 149–171. https://doi.org/10.1093/applin/amq037.

MacIntyre, P. D., MacKay, E., Ross, J., & Abel, E. (2017). The emerging need for methods appropriate to study dynamic systems. In L. Ortega & Z. Han (Eds.), *Complexity theory and language development: In celebration of Diane Larsen-Freeman* (pp. 97–122). John Benjamins.

MacIntyre, P. D., Noels, K. A., & Clément, R. (1997). Biases in self-ratings of second language proficiency: The role of language anxiety. *Language Learning, 47*(2), 265–287. https://doi.org/10.1111/0023-8333.81997008.

MacKinnon, D. P. (2008). *Introduction to statistical mediation analysis*. Taylor & Francis Group.

Malmkjær, K. (Ed.). (2010). *The Routledge linguistics encyclopedia* (3rd ed.). Routledge.

Martin, J. R., & White, P. R. R. (2005). *The language of evaluation, appraisal in English*. Palgrave Macmillan.

McCroskey, J. C., & Baer, J. E. (1985). *Willingness to communicate: The construct and its measurement*. Paper presented at the Speech Communication Association Convention, Denver, CO.

McCroskey, J. C., & Richmond, V. P. (1982). Communication apprehension and shyness: Conceptual and operational distinctions. *Central States Speech Journal, 33*(3), 458–468. https://doi.org/10.1080/10510978209388452.

McCroskey, J. C., & Richmond, V. P. (1987). Willingness to communicate. In J. C. McCroskey & J. A. Daly (Eds.), *Personality and interpersonal communication* (pp. 129–156). Sage.

McCroskey, J. C., & Richmond, V. P. (1991). Willingness to communicate: A cognitive view. In M. Booth-Butterfield (Ed.), *Communication, cognition, and anxiety* (pp. 19–37). Sage.

McCroskey, L. L., & McCroskey, J. C. (2002). Willingness to communicate and communication apprehension in the classroom. In J. L. Chesebro & J. C. McCroskey (Eds.), *Communication for teachers* (pp. 19–34). Allyn & Bacon.

Menezes, E., & Juan-Garau, M. (2015). English learners' willingness to communicate and achievement in CLIL and formal instruction contexts. In M. Juan-Garau & J. Salazar-Noguera (Eds.), *Content-based language learning in multilingual educational environments* (pp. 221–236). Springer.

Merriam-Webster. (n.d.). *Merriam-Webster.com dictionary.* July 18, 2023, www.merriamwebster.com/.

Morell, T. (2018). Multimodal competence and effective interactive lecturing. *System, 77,* 70–79. https://doi.org/10.1016/j.system.2017.12.006.

Mortensen, C. D., Arntson, P. H., & Lustig, M. (1977). The measurement of verbal predispositions: Scale development and application. *Human Communication Research, 3*(2), 146–158. https://doi.org/10.1111/j.1468-2958.1977.tb00513.x.

Multimodal Analysis Company. (2013). *Multimodal Analysis Video* [Computer software].

Munezane, Y. (2015). Enhancing willingness to communicate: Relative effects of visualization and goal setting. *The Modern Language Journal, 99*(1), 175–191. https://doi.org/10.1111/modl.12193.

Mystkowska-Wiertelak, A., & Pawlak, M. (2017). *Willingness to communicate in instructed second language acquisition: Combining a macro- and micro-perspective.* Multilingual Matters.

Nematizadeh, S., & Cao, Y. (Katherine). (2023). Investigating willingness to communicate in synchronous group discussion tasks: One step closer towards authentic communication. *International Review of Applied Linguistics in Language Teaching,* Advance online publication. https://doi .org/10.1515/iral-2022-0092.

Nematizadeh, S., & Wood, D. (2019). Willingness to communicate and second language speech fluency: An investigation of affective and cognitive dynamics. *The Canadian Modern Language Review, 73*(3), 197–215. https://doi.org/10.3138/cmlr.2017-0146.

Nitta, R., & Baba, K. (2015). Self-regulation in the evolution of the ideal L2 self: A complex dynamic systems approach to the L2 motivational self system. In Z. Dörnyei, P. D. MacIntyre, & A. Henry (Eds.), *Motivational dynamics in language learning* (pp. 367–396). Multilingual Matters.

O'Halloran, K. L. (2005). *Mathematical discourse: Language, symbolism and visual images*. Continuum.

O'Halloran, K. L. (2011). Multimodal discourse analysis. In K. Hyland & B. Paltridge (Eds.), *Companion to discourse* (pp. 120–137). Continuum.

O'Laughlin, K. D., Martin, M. J., & Ferrer, E. (2018). Cross-sectional analysis of longitudinal mediation processes. *Multivariate Behavioral Research, 53* (3), 375–402. https://doi.org/10.1080/00273171.2018.1454822.

Pawlak, M., & Mystkowska-Wiertelak, A. (2015). Investigating the dynamic nature of L2 willingness to communicate. *System, 50*, 1–9. https://doi.org/ 10.1016/j.system.2015.02.001.

Pawlak, M., Mystkowska-Wiertelak, A., & Bielak, J. (2016). Investigating the nature of classroom willingness to communicate (WTC): A micro-perspective. *Language Teaching Research, 20*(5), 654–671. https://doi.org/10.1177/ 1362168815609615.

Pekrun, R. (2006). The control-value theory of achievement emotions: Assumptions, corollaries, and implications for educational research and practice. *Educational Psychology Review, 18*(4), 315–341. https://doi.org/ 10.1007/s10648-006-9029-9.

Peng, J. (2007). Willingness to communicate in the Chinese EFL classroom: A cultural perspective. In J. Liu (Ed.), *English language teaching in China: New approaches, perspectives, and standards* (pp. 250–269). Continuum.

Peng, J. (2012). Towards an ecological understanding of willingness to communicate in EFL classrooms in China. *System, 40*(2), 203–213. https://doi .org/10.1016/j.system.2012.02.002.

Peng, J. (2014). *Willingness to communicate in the Chinese EFL university classroom: An ecological perspective*. Multilingual Matters.

Peng, J. (2015). L2 motivational self system, attitudes, and affect as predictors of L2 WTC: An imagined community perspective. *The Asia-Pacific Education Researcher, 24*(2), 433–443. https://doi.org/10.1007/s40299- 014-0195-0.

Peng, J. (2019a). The roles of multimodal pedagogic effects and classroom environment in willingness to communicate in English. *System, 82*, 161–173. https://doi.org/10.1016/j.system.2019.04.006.

Peng, J. (2019b). Understanding willingness to communicate as embedded in classroom multimodal affordances: Evidence from interdisciplinary perspectives. *Linguistics and Education, 51*, 59–68. https://doi.org/10.1016/j.linged .2019.04.006.

Peng, J. (2020a). Teacher interaction strategies and situated willingness to communicate. *ELT Journal*, *74*(3), 307–317. https://doi.org/10.1093/elt/ccaa012.

Peng, J. (2020b). Willing silence and silent willingness to communicate (WTC) in the Chinese EFL classroom: A dynamic systems perspective. In J. King & S. Harumi (Eds.), *East Asian perspectives on silence in English language education* (pp. 143–165). Multilingual Matters.

Peng, J. (2021). *Approaching willingness to communicate (WTC) in English from interdisciplinary perspectives: Convergent and divergent evidence* [Paper presentation]. April 23–25, ELC Conference 2021, Shantou, Guangdong, China.

Peng, J. (2022). Willingness to communicate. In S. Li, P. Hiver & M. Papi (Eds.), *The Routledge handbook of second language acquisition and individual differences* (pp. 159–171). Routledge.

Peng, J., & Wang, Z. (2024). The predictive roles of enjoyment, anxiety, willingness to communicate on students' performance in English public speaking classes. *International Review of Applied Linguistics in Language Teaching*, *62*, 485–508. https://doi.org/10.1515/iral-2022-0162.

Peng, J., & Woodrow, L. J. (2010). Willingness to communicate in English: A model in Chinese EFL classroom context. *Language Learning*, *60*(4), 834–876. https://doi.org/10.1111/j.1467-9922.2010.00576.x.

Peng, J., & Wu, L. (2022). Motivational profiles of Chinese university students majoring in Spanish: A comparative study. *Journal of Multilingual and Multicultural Development*, Advance online publication. https://doi.org/10.1080/01434632.2022.2035740.

Peng, J., Zhang, L., & Chen, Y. (2017). The mediation of multimodal affordances on willingness to communicate in the English as a foreign language classroom. *TESOL Quarterly*, *51*(2), 302–331. https://doi.org/10.1002/tesq.298.

Reinders, H., & Wattana, S. (2015). Affect and willingness to communicate in digital game-based learning. *ReCALL*, *27*(1), 38–57. https://doi.org/10.1017/S0958344014000226.

Ro, E., & Burch, A. R. (2020). Willingness to communicate/participate' in action: A case study of changes in a recipient's practices in an L2 book club. *Linguistics and Education*, *58*, Article 100821. https://doi.org/10.1016/j.linged.2020.100821.

Sato, M., & Dussuel Lam, C. (2021). Metacognitive instruction with young learners: A case of willingness to communicate, L2 use, and metacognition of oral communication. *Language Teaching Research*, *25*(6), 899–921. https://doi.org/10.1177/13621688211004639.

Seligman, M. E. P., & Csikszentmihalyi, M. (2000). Positive psychology: An introduction. *American Psychologist, 55*(1), 5–14. https://doi.org/10.1037/0003-066X.55.1.5.

Shen, X., Hao, C., & Peng, J. (2022). Promoting EFL learners' willingness to communicate through transmediation in a digital storytelling workshop. *Journal of Multilingual and Multicultural Development, 45*(8), 3109–3126. https://doi.org/10.1080/01434632.2022.2086257.

Shen, X., Shen, X., & Peng, J. (2024). Digital storytelling: A literacy-building tool to promote willingness to communicate in a second language. *RELC Journal, 55*(3), 819–826. https://doi.org/10.1177/00336882231157461.

Skehan, P. (1989). *Individual differences in second language learning*. Edward Arnold.

Taherian, T., Shirvan, M. E., Yazdanmehr, E., Kruk, M., & Pawlak, M. (2023). A longitudinal analysis of informal digital learning of English, willingness to communicate and foreign language boredom: A latent change score mediation model. *The Asia-Pacific Education Researcher*, Advance online publication. https://doi.org/10.1007/s40299-023-00751-z.

Tai, T.-Y. (2024). Comparing the effects of intelligent personal assistant-human and human-human interactions on EFL learners' willingness to communicate beyond the classroom. *Computers & Education, 210*, Article 104965. https://doi.org/10.1016/j.compedu.2023.104965.

Tai, T.-Y., & Chen, H. H.-J. (2023). The impact of Google Assistant on adolescent EFL learners' willingness to communicate. *Interactive Learning Environments, 31*(3), 1485–1502. https://doi.org/10.1080/10494820.2020.1841801.

Tan, S. (2005). A systemic functional approach to the analysis of corporate television advertisements [Unpublished master's thesis]. National University of Singapore.

Tavakoli, E., & Davoudi, M. (2017). Willingness to communicate orally: The case of Iranian EFL learners. *Journal of Psycholinguistic Research, 46*(6), 1509–1527. https://doi.org/10.1007/s10936-017-9504-0.

Tavakoli, M., & Zarrinabadi, N. (2018). Differential effects of explicit and implicit corrective feedback on EFL learners' willingness to communicate. *Innovation in Language Learning and Teaching, 12*(3), 247–259. https://doi.org/10.1080/17501229.2016.1195391.

Teimouri, Y. (2017). L2 selves, emotions, and motivated behaviors. *Studies in Second Language Acquisition, 39*(4), 681–709. https://doi.org/10.1017/S0272263116000243.

Ushioda, E. (2009). A person-in-context relational view of emergent motivation, self and identity. In Z. Dörnyei & E. Ushioda (Eds.), *Motivation, language identity and the L2 self* (pp. 315–228). Multilingual Matters.

van Lier, L. (2002). An ecological-semiotic perspective on language and linguistics. In C. Kramsch (Ed.), *Language acquisition and language socialization: Ecological perspectives* (pp. 140–164). Continuum.

Verspoor, M. H., de Bot, K., & Lowie, W. (Eds.). (2011). *A dynamic approach to second languagedevelopment: Methods and techniques* (Vol. 29). John Benjamins.

Vinogradova, P., Linville, H. A., & Bickel, B. (2011). "Listen to my story and you will know me": Digital stories as student-centered collaborative projects. *TESOL Journal, 2*(2), 173–202. https://doi.org/10.5054/tj.2011.250380.

Wang, H., Peng, A., & Patterson, M. M. (2021). The roles of class social climate, language mindset, and emotions in predicting willingness to communicate in a foreign language. *System, 99*, Article 102529. https://doi.org/10.1016/j.system.2021.102529.

Weaver, C. (2005). Using the Rasch model to develop a measure of second language learners' willingness to communicate within a language classroom. *Journal of Applied Measurement, 6*(4), 396–415.

Wei, L. (2018). Translanguaging as a practical theory of language. *Applied Linguistics, 39*(1), 9–30. https://doi.org/10.1093/applin/amx039.

Wei, W., & Cao, Y. (2021). Willing, silent or forced participation? Insights from English for academic purposes classrooms. *RELC Journal*, Advance online publication. https://doi.org/10.1177/00336882211066619.

Wen, W. P., & Clément, R. (2003). A Chinese conceptualisation of willingness to communicate in ESL. *Language, Culture and Curriculum, 16*(1), 18–38. https://doi.org/10.1080/07908310308666654.

Wood, D. (2016). Willingness to communicate and second language speech fluency: An idiodynamic investigation. *System, 60*, 11–28. https://doi.org/10.1016/j.system.2016.05.003.

Yang, L. (2018). Higher education expansion and post-college unemployment: Understanding the roles of fields of study in China. *International Journal of Educational Development, 62*, 62–74. https://doi.org/10.1016/j.ijedudev.2018.02.009.

Yang, X., & Yin, S. (2022). Interpersonal projection as EFL teachers' discourse strategy to enhance students' willingness to communicate: A systemic-functional perspective. *System, 104*, Article 102687. https://doi.org/10.1016/j.system.2021.102687.

Yashima, T. (2002). Willingness to communicate in a second language: The Japanese EFL context. *The Modern Language Journal, 86*(1), 54–66. https://doi.org/10.1111/1540-4781.00136.

Yashima, T. (2009). International posture and the ideal L2 self in the Japanese EFL context. In Z. Dörnyei & E. Ushioda (Eds.), *Motivation, language identity and the L2 self* (pp. 144–192). Multilingual Matters.

Yashima, T. (2022). Willingness to communicate in an L2. In T. Gregersen & S. Mercer (Eds.), *The Routledge handbook of the psychology of language learning and teaching* (pp. 260–271). Routledge.

Yashima, T., MacIntyre, P. D., & Ikeda, M. (2018). Situated willingness to communicate in an L2: Interplay of individual characteristics and context. *Language Teaching Research, 22*(1), 115–137. https://doi.org/10.1177/1362168816657851.

Yashima, T., & Zenuk-Nishide, L. (2008). The impact of learning contexts on proficiency, attitudes, and L2 communication: Creating an imagined international community. *System, 36*(4), 566–585. https://doi.org/10.1016/j.system.2008.03.006.

Yashima, T., Zenuk-Nishide, L., & Shimizu, K. (2004). The influence of attitudes and affect on willingness to communicate and second language communication. *Language Learning, 54*(1), 119–152. https://doi.org/10.1111/j.1467-9922.2004.00250.x.

Yi, Y., Shin, D., & Cimasko, T. (2020). Special issue: Multimodal composing in multilingual learning and teaching contexts. *Journal of Second Language Writing, 47*, Article 100717. https://doi.org/10.1016/j.jslw.2020.100717.

Yu, M. (2015). An examination of the dynamic feature of WTC through dyadic group interaction. *System, 55*, 11–20. https://doi.org/10.1016/j.system.2015.08.001.

Yue, Z. (2014). Chinese university students' willingness to communicate in the L2 classroom: The complex and dynamic interplay of self-concept, future self-guides and the sociocultural context. In K. Csizér & M. Magid (Eds.), *The impact of self-concept on language learning* (pp. 250–267). Multilingual Matters.

Zabihi, R., Ghominejad, S., & Javad Ahmadian, M. (2021). Can willingness to communicate, communication in English anxiety, behavioural inhibition and behavioural action predict perceived L2 fluency? *Language Teaching Research*, Advance online publication. https://doi.org/10.1177/13621688211044071.

Zare, M., Shooshtari, Z. G., & Jalilifar, A. (2022). The interplay of oral corrective feedback and L2 willingness to communicate across proficiency levels. *Language Teaching Research, 26*(6), 1158–1178. https://doi.org/10.1177/1362168820928967.

Zarrinabadi, N. (2014). Communicating in a second language: Investigating the effect of teacher on learners' willingness to communicate. *System, 42*, 288–295. https://doi.org/10.1016/j.system.2013.12.014.

Zarrinabadi, N., Lou, N. M., & Shirzad, M. (2021). Autonomy support predicts language mindsets: Implications for developing communicative competence and willingness to communicate in EFL classrooms. *Learning and Individual Differences, 86,* Article 101981. https://doi.org/10.1016/j.lindif.2021.101981.

Zhang, J., Beckmann, N., & Beckmann, J. F. (2018). To talk or not to talk: A review of situational antecedents of willingness to communicate in the second language classroom. *System, 72,* 226–239. https://doi.org/10.1016/j.system.2018.01.003.

Zhang, J., Beckmann, N., & Beckmann, J. F. (2020). More than meets the ear: Individual differences in trait and state willingness to communicate as predictors of language learning performance in a Chinese EFL context. *Language Teaching Research,* Advance online publication. https://doi.org/10.1177/1362168820951931.

Zhang, C., Meng, Y., & Ma, X. (2024). Artificial intelligence in EFL speaking: Impact on enjoyment, anxiety, and willingness to communicate. *System, 121,* Article 103259. https://doi.org/10.1016/j.system.2024.103259.

Zhang, L. J., Saeedian, A., & Fathi, J. (2022). Testing a model of growth mindset, ideal L2 self, boredom, and WTC in an EFL context. *Journal of Multilingual and Multicultural Development,* Advance online publication. https://doi.org/10.1080/01434632.2022.2100893.

Zhong, Q. (2013). Understanding Chinese learners' willingness to communicate in a New Zealand ESL classroom: A multiple case study drawing on the theory of planned behavior. *System, 41*(3), 740–751. https://doi.org/10.1016/j.system.2013.08.001.

Zhou, Q. (2023a). Investigating willingness to communicate vis-à-vis learner talk in a low-proficiency EAP classroom in the UK study-abroad context. *International Review of Applied Linguistics in Language Teaching,* Advance online publication. https://doi.org/10.1515/iral-2022-0219.

Zhou, Q. (2023b). Translating willingness to communicate into learner talk in a Chinese as a foreign language (CFL) classroom. *Language Teaching Research,* Advance online publication. https://doi.org/10.1177/13621688231176035.

Acknowledgment

This publication was financially supported by the Li Ka Shing Foundation.

Cambridge Elements ⁼

Language Teaching

Heath Rose

University of Oxford

Heath Rose is Professor of Applied Linguistics at the University of Oxford and Deputy Director (People) of the Department of Education. Before moving into academia, Heath worked as a language teacher in Australia and Japan in both school and university contexts. He is author of numerous books, such as *Introducing Global Englishes, The Japanese Writing System, Data Collection Research Methods in Applied Linguistics,* and *Global Englishes for Language Teaching.*

Jim McKinley

University College London

Jim McKinley is Professor of Applied Linguistics at IOE Faculty of Education and Society, University College London. He has taught in higher education in the UK, Japan, Australia, and Uganda, as well as US schools. His research targets implications of globalization for L2 writing, language education, and higher education studies, particularly the teaching-research nexus and English medium instruction. Jim is co-author and co-editor of several books on research methods in applied linguistics. He is an Editor-in-Chief of the journal System.

About the Series

This Elements series aims to close the gap between researchers and practitioners by allying research with language teaching practices, in its exploration of research informed teaching, and teaching-informed research. The series builds upon a rich history of pedagogical research in its exploration of new insights within the field of language teaching.

Cambridge Elements ☰

Language Teaching

Printed in the United States
by Baker & Taylor Publisher Services